Anonymous

The advantages of Richmond, Virginia, as a manufacturing and trading centre

Anonymous

The advantages of Richmond, Virginia, as a manufacturing and trading centre

ISBN/EAN: 9783337563202

Printed in Europe, USA, Canada, Australia, Japan

Cover: Foto ©Andreas Hilbeck / pixelio.de

More available books at **www.hansebooks.com**

THE ADVANTAGES

OF

RICHMOND,

VIRGINIA,

AS A

Manufacturing & Trading

CENTRE,

WITH NOTES FOR THE GUIDANCE OF TOURISTS
ON THE LINES OF TRANSPORTATION
RUNNING FROM RICHMOND.

RICHMOND:
PUBLISHED UNDER THE AUSPICES OF THE TRADE COMMITTEES OF
THE CHAMBER OF COMMERCE AND COMMERCIAL CLUB.
1882.

WM. ELLIS JONES,
PRINTER,
RICHMOND, VA.

TO THE READER:

The wonderful development of the great West is very largely due to the aid afforded by the men and money of New England and the East. It is believed that the time has come when the men and money of New England and the East can find as rich returns in Southern development. In this view the good people of Richmond present this little book, and they ask for its contents a patient consideration.

CONTENTS.

CHAPTER I.—*Richmond, Virginia:*   *Page.*

    Settlement—Topography—Health—Public Grounds and Parks—Inter-Communication—Churches—Schools and Colleges—Temper of People, &c.................................. 5-10

CHAPTER II.—*Means of Transportation:*

    The Past and the Present—The Various Railroad Systems—The Country Drained by Them—Water Communication... 11-21

CHAPTER III.—*General Manufacturing Exhibit:*

    Capital Invested—Hands Employed—Aggregate Sales—Special Advantages—Water and Steam Power—Labor Supply—Raw Material Available—Fostering Auxiliaries.. 22-29

CHAPTER IV.—*Manufactures in Detail:*

    The Banking Basis — The Coal Movement — The Iron Interest—Milling—A Comprehensive Range of Industries... 30-45

CHAPTER V.—*The Jobbing Trade:*

    How It Has Been Built Up — Richmond the Closest, Cheapest, and Most Natural Market for the South—List of Jobbing Enterprises—Some Potent Reasons Why the Trade Will Continue to Increase.................. 46-49

CHAPTER VI.—*Of Interest to Tourists:*

    Historic—Points of Interest in the City—As a Home for Invalids—The Scenery on the Railroad Lines and the Summer Resorts... 50-64

Richmond, Virginia.

CHAPTER I.

SETTLEMENT—TOPOGRAPHY—HEALTH—PUBLIC GROUNDS AND PARKS — INTER-COMMUNICATION — CHURCHES— SCHOOLS AND COLLEGES—TEMPER OF PEOPLE, &c.

Richmond, the capital city of Virginia, was settled in 1609 by a small body of colonists sent out from Jamestown, but for a long period it was little more than an outpost on the then frontier. In 1737 it was laid off in streets and lots by Colonel William Byrd, was duly incorporated in 1742, and became the seat of government in 1779. It is situated at the head of navigation and tidewater, on James river, 74 miles in an air line from the sea; 150 miles by the river. Latitude 30°, 32', 17", N.; longitude 77°, 27', 28", W.

TOPOGRAPHY.

Topographically considered, the city is built upon two undulating plateaux, resting on granite, divided by the valley of Shockoe creek, and again subdivided by smaller valleys and ravines, through one of which flows Gillie's creek. This latter stream may be said to divide the eastern plateau proper from another plateau extending into the country. The general appearance of the city, particularly from the river front, which is 2.06 miles in length between the eastern and western corporation limits, is hilly. The principal streets are laid off from east to west, parallel with the river; the cross streets from north to south, the blocks being rectangular and for the most part of uniform area. The lowest sections of the city range from 15 to 40 feet, and the highest from 150 to 200 feet, above tide level. The corporation area, as at present bounded, embraces 6.12 square miles.

RICHMOND, VIRGINIA.

Its greatest length from east to west is 3.50 miles; from north to south, 1.75 miles. The pavements are from 10 to 12 feet in width.

HEALTH AND DRAINAGE.

In point of health Richmond has every natural advantage. The mean temperature for the year 1881 was 61°, and its elevation above the sea secures it a constancy of pure air. Total rainfall (1881), 38.64 inches; average for eleven years 37.37 inches. Even at the highest range of the thermometer sunstroke is very rare, and seldom fatal. The undulating and rolling character of the surface, producing short divides between the valleys of the creeks and the ravines, render it easily drained by its 18.35 miles of main sewerage already completed. As building extends the drainage and grading extends with it.

PUBLIC GROUNDS AND PARKS.

The total area of the public grounds and parks in the city proper is above 40 acres—divided into five principal parks and a number of smaller open spaces. Chimborazo Park, 29, and Libby Hill Park, 3.50 acres, are located in the eastern portion of the city, 150 feet above tide level. They command a view of the city of Manchester on the opposite side of the river, together with the bridges connecting it and Richmond; the lower James and its tortuous and picturesque windings for miles; the falls above the city, the docks and wharves, and the rich lowgrounds of Chesterfield county. The Capitol Park, 13 acres, with its ancient State-house, its statuary, its parade ground, and beautiful foliage, is like 'Boston Common, the centre of the city, and promises to continue the point from which extensions will be made in all available directions. Gamble's Hill Park, 8.50 acres, is on the south and river front of the city, overlooking many of the principal manufacturing establishments, and also commanding a view of Manchester, the lower James, Belle Isle, and the smaller islands that stud the river at and above the falls. Monroe Park, 8.875 acres, is in the western extension of the city—a level plat, well shaded and beautifully ornamented with beds of shrubs and flowers. Just on the western edge of the city are the Old Reservoir grounds—a most attractive place, —and a mile further west is the New Reservoir Park. This latter embraces 160 acres, bordering on the upper reach of the James, and is the driving park of the Richmond people. Here are located the New Reservoir and the New Pump Houses. The drives are kept in fine condition, and in the course of a few years the entire area will be thoroughly shaded. One of its present principal attractions is a large lake, used for boating in the summer and skating in the winter. It is also used as a fish-hatchery, and is one of a projected cordon of lakes to be extended to the river, the last of which will, in certain seasons, be at the service of anglers.

INTER-COMMUNICATION.

Communication between the different parts of the city is easy and convenient. A double-street railway track traverses the two principal thoroughfares—Main and Broad streets—from east to west, with the prospect of several cross lines, and a further extension west, as improvements may demand. With the street-car facilities now afforded, access from the line to most any part of the city requires only a few minutes walk.

GAS AND WATER SUPPLY.

The city is well lighted by gas, of its own manufacture, and is now abundantly supplied with water from James river, the purity of which is well attested both by the experience of the people and chemical analysis. The water is pumped from several stations along the upper river front, or falls, above navigation, which renders it free from pollution of any character whatever, and into reservoirs, dividing the distribution into two services. The maximum pumping capacity is 24,000,000 of gallons per day, and the total storage capacity of the reservoirs 52,000,000 of gallons. The city authorities, realizing that rapid growth in population and manufactures could not be assured except with an ample supply of water, made the splendid provision for it above described. The fire department is paid by the city, and is efficient both as to apparatus and the men composing it.

CHURCH EDIFICES AND MEMBERSHIP.

It has been frequently remarked, with a great deal of truth, by strangers visiting the city, that it is the "greatest church-going place of its size in the United States." The church statistics for 1881 make the following exhibit. Number of edifices 55, divided as follows: Baptist, white, 9, colored, 10; Catholic, 3; Disciples or Christians, 2; Episcopal, white, 9, colored, 1; Friends, 1; German Evangelical, 1; Hebrew, 3; Lutheran, 2; Methodist, white, 8, colored, 2; Presbyterian, 4; total membership 30,146, or but a fraction less than one-half of the entire population, which, according to the census of 1880, was 63,600. The total number of children in Sunday schools was 14,893. Since these figures were compiled several new congregations have been organized. Some of the church edifices are exceedingly handsome, and connected with all the denominations are working and effective benevolent organizations.

SCHOOLS AND COLLEGES.

The educational facilities are unsurpassed. The free schools are thirteen in number, grading from the high school to the primary, and in accommodations, teaching ability, and the general supervision given them, compare most favorably with any free schools in any city North or South—a fact fully attested by leading educators from other States. In 1881 the total number of teachers in service was 146;—scholars, 5,995. The private schools of all grades are abundant. Richmond College, and the Virginia Medical College, together with several large female institutes are also located here. Besides this the city is within a days' ride of all the leading institutions of learning in the State. The Virginia Military Institute and Washington and Lee University at Lexington; the University of Virginia, near Charlottesville; William and Mary College at Williamsburg; Hampden Sidney College, and Union Theological Seminary, near Farmville; Roanoke College, at Salem; Randolph Macon College, at Ashland, and the several female seminaries and male academies at Petersburg, Staunton, Danville and other points.

AS A HOME FOR ARTIZANS.

Few cities can offer greater inducements than Richmond as a home for artizans. In addition to its school and church privileges and its healthy location, it presents unusual facilities for enabling the thrifty to buy their own houses. In nearly every

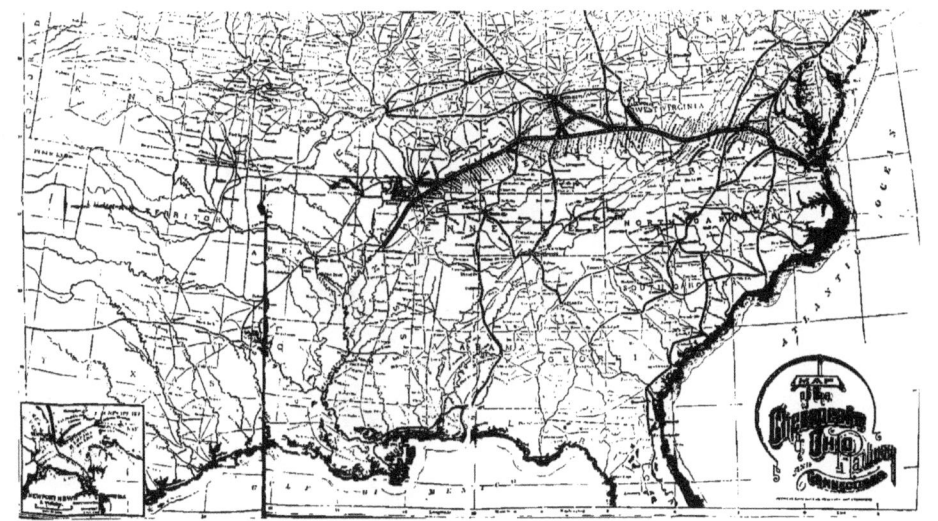

direction in which the city is extending there are desirable building lots which can be bought cheap, and are convenient to the manufacturing plants that have been or may be made. The means of enjoyment in the city are ample—all the respectable benevolent orders are in good condition, and wages in proportion to the cost of living are higher than in many northern cities. The tenement-house system, with the stifling atmosphere of narrow streets and cramped courts is practically unknown and unnecessary. Besides having the parks as "breathing places" in warm weather, it is hardly possible to walk a half dozen blocks in any direction in the city without coming in sight of running water and green fields. The city is beautifully shaded with linden, maple, and other choice trees.

COST OF LIVING.

During the present year there has been a slight advance in rents, owing to the unusual demand for houses. But this is compensated for in the low price of necessary articles of living. All the railroads leading into the city run through thickly wooded sections of the State, and all save one have coal fields on their line. In the matter of fuel alone it is safe to assert there is a difference of fifty cents per ton in coal at retail in favor of Richmond consumers the year round, as compared with northern trade centres. In wood there is about four times this margin. Live stock raising is a large industry in the western and southwestern portions of the State particularly, and the price of meats averages much below the cost in cities north of us. In vegetables, owing to the fact that the surrounding country is one vast market garden, the price is reduced almost to a minimum. The fish and oyster supply is unlimited, and is accessible by both the York and the James rivers. Shad run to our very wharves, and the river above the city is well stocked with game fishes. From the mountains, in season, is brought a plentiful supply of venison. To revert to the matter of rents, however, as before indicated, on all the suburbs there are most advantageous building sites to be purchased cheaply, and which, it may be added, offer inducements to build, not only for individual occupancy, but for rental. In view of the abundance of brick-clay, granite, timber and other material used in building, contiguous to the city, capital could find no better investment than in small houses for artizans and others in moderate circumstances. It is demonstrable, considering the low price of ground, that a given number of such houses, which in Philadelphia, for instance, would yield from three to four per cent. upon the investment, would in Richmond yield six or seven per cent.

CHARACTER OF THE PEOPLE.

The people of Richmond are notably law-abiding and hospitable. To strangers they show every courtesy, business and social, and are ever ready to extend a warm welcome to any who may desire to settle in their midst. There are three large clubs, the Commercial, the Richmond and the Westmoreland, and several minor clubs, the doors of which are open to all visitors who may be properly introduced, and where the best elements of business and society circles are met with.

PUBLICATIONS AND LIBRARY FACILITIES.

There are five daily papers in Richmond—the *Dispatch*, the *Whig*, the *Staats-Gazette*, the *Zietung*, (the two latter German), morning, and the *State*, evening. The religious papers are, the *Central Presbyterian*, the *Southern Churchman* (Episcopal), the *Catholic Visitor*, the *Christian Advocate* (Methodist), and the *Religious Herald* (Baptist). The periodicals are the *Virginia Medical Monthly*, the *Southern Clinic*, the *Southern Planter*, the *Southern Pulpit*, the *Southern Historical Society Papers*, and the *Virginia Educational Journal*. There are also several literary, news and trade weeklies, including the *Industrial South*, the *Commercial and Tobacco Leaf*, *Every Saturday*, the *Star*, and the *Trade Journal and Hotel Reporter*. The library facilities are the State, the Court of Appeals, the Young Men's Christian Association, the Richmond College, and several smaller libraries. The principal places of amusement are the Richmond Theatre and Mozart Hall, and a joint stock company is being formed to erect a handsome Opera House. The Mozart Association was organized as a glee club several years ago, and now has five hundred contributing members. Concerts or parlor operas, in which are engaged the best amateur and professional musical talent in the city, are given weekly.

CHAPTER II.

MEANS OF TRANSPORTATION.

THE PAST AND THE PRESENT—THE VARIOUS RAILROAD SYSTEMS—THE COUNTRY DRAINED BY THEM—WATER COMMUNICATION.

Before presenting the claims and advantages of Richmond as a commercial and manufacturing centre, there are several points to be submitted in anticipation of the obvious question, "Why has not progress in these directions been more rapid?" This is easily accounted for. When the facts are weighed, it will, we are confident, be admitted that under the circumstances the city's recuperation and development have been unprecedented. Virginia, in common with the South in general, was, prior to the war, an agricultural country by distinction. The comfort of the people was so universal, that there was little disposition to embark much in manufactures, or any business conducted on a large scale, except as hereinafter noted. With the abolition of slavery, bearing as it did so severely upon the farming interest, the energies of the people had to be directed to new callings. The accommodation to this state of things was necessarily gradual, yet our men are now found in every line of business; and it is not too much to assert that what has already been accomplished gives promise of a splendid future. As for Richmond itself, seventeen years ago the whole business portion was in ashes and without insurance. The principle streets were impassable for vehicles, and the people were without a medium of exchange. Utter ruin, financially, was the rule. What capital could be borrowed, or in any way realized from the wreck, had to be invested in rebuilding, or in business ventures, which, through immediate demand, would insure the quickest profit. Business men had literally to begin at the bottom, and, what is more, become used to a manner of doing business which was entirely new to their experience. Further, until within the last few years, railroad connections were incomplete, as far as any extended territory for profitable distribution was concerned, and what territory was accessible was barred against Richmond trade by the railroad discriminations in favor of other points. Every influence that could be exerted, was exerted to the utmost to drive the Southern trade to cities further north. The task of overcoming these obstacles was a herculean one, but will and energy have accomplished it. Steadily and conservatively business has been pushed until, against the condition of affairs above cited, Richmond shows to-day, a business quarter handsomely and substantially rebuilt, a credit that would be an honor to any community, an immense and constantly increasing wholesale trade, and a manufacturing interest which, in 1881, was represented by nearly $33,000,000 of sales. The enterprise, business tact, and public spirit of the people have finally compelled a recognition of the importance of the city as a distributing centre for the South and West, and the result is that it is the point of radiation for six railroads, which separately or as parts of great trunk lines or systems, bring it in connection with and ramify every portion of the Union. From the wharves in Rocketts, and from Newports News, and West Point—deep water outlets for and tributaries to Richmond commerce,—there are also facilities for reaching by both sailing vessels and steamers all the important home and foreign ports. In order to convey an adequate idea of the relations of Richmond to the fields of trade demand and supply, let us take a brief glance at the railroad systems and other lines of transportion centering here.

RICHMOND AND DANVILLE RAILROAD SYSTEM.

This system (see accompanying map) controls through ownership and lease 2,006.50 miles of trackage, as follows: Richmond and Danville Railroad, main line and branches, Richmond to Danville, Va., 152 miles; Piedmont Railroad, Danville, Va., to Greensboro, N. C., 49 miles; North Carolina Railroad, Goldsboro to Charlotte, N. C., 223 miles; North Western North Carolina Railroad, Greensboro to Salem, N. C., 25 miles; Charlotte,

Columbia and Augusta Railroad, Charlotte, N. C., to Augusta, Ga., 191 miles; Western North Carolina Railroad, Salisbury, N. C., to Paint Rock, Tenn., 186 miles; Columbia and Greensville Railroad and branches, Columbia, S. C., to Greensville, S. C., 296 miles; Knoxville and Augusta Railroad, Knoxville, Tenn., to Maysville, Tenn., 16 miles; Atlanta and Charlotte Air-Line Railway, Charlotte, N. C., to Atlanta, Ga., 288 miles; North Eastern Railroad of Georgia, Lulu, Ga., to Athens, Ga., 40 miles; Elberton Air-Line Railway, Elberton, Ga., to Toccoa, Ga., 51 miles; Spartansburg and Ashville Railroad, Spartansburg, S. C., to Henderson, N. C., 50 miles; Richmond, York River and Chesapeake Railroad, Richmond to West Point, Va., 39 miles; Virginia Midland Railway, Danville, Va., to Alexandria, Va., 400.50 miles. From Richmond the line passes through the coalfields and granite formations of Chesterfield, crossing the Norfolk and Western (from Norfolk *via* Farmville and Lynchburg, and onward through southwestern Virginia) at Burkeville. Thence almost in a direct line through the grain and tobacco districts to Danville—the terminus of the old main line. At Danville it connects with the Virginia Midland north. Southwardly the system extends over the North Carolina Railroad to Charlotte, N. C., thence dividing, with one line to Augusta, Ga., and the other to Atlanta, Ga. From Atlanta, Ga., the line under construction is projected through Birmingham and the Black Warrior coal-fields of North Alabama, across the Mississippi river to Texarcana, Texas, to connect at that point with the Texas, Mexican and California Railroad lines.

In North Carolina and South Carolina the system intersects the leading lines, finished and projected, from east to west, its cross lines and feeders draining the entire Piedmont sections, not only of Virginia, but of North Carolina and South Carolina, bringing the principal towns and cities in these sections some two hundred miles nearer to Richmond than to any Northern city seeking Southern trade. The system runs, also in the most direct route through the fine tobacco district of North Carolina, and the great cotton belts of South Carolina and Georgia, and has under natural tribute for outlet the inexhaustible mineral deposits of the three latter States, together with the products of their forests. The Western North Carolina railroad from Salisbury, on the main stem to Paint Rock, Tennessee, from which point it is projected to Morristown, in that State, is an especially important feeder, opening up, not only the most picturesque portion of North Carolina, but a most valuable country both in point of agricultural and mineral products. It is especially a region of marbles of all shades. At Richmond and West Point the system has water connection with all the principal Northern ports, and wharfage capacity and depth of water sufficient for direct shipment to all foreign countries.

CHESAPEAKE AND OHIO RAILWAY SYSTEM.

The Chesapeake and Ohio system proper (see map) has under trackage 1,121 miles—Chesapeake and Ohio railway, Richmond, Va., to Huntington, West Va , 420 miles; Newports News line, Richmond to Newports News, 75 miles; Elizabethtown, Lexington and Big Sandy railway, Huntington, West Va., to Lexington, Ky., 140 miles; Louisville and Nashville railroad, Lexington, Ky., to Louisville, Ky., 94 miles; Chesapeake and Ohio and Southwest railway, Louisville, Ky., to Memphis, Tenn., 392 miles. At Memphis it connects with the Memphis and Little Rock railroad to Little Rock, where connection is made with Gould's system to El Paso, on the Southern Pacific, running through to San Francisco, Cal., and giving the most direct route to the Golden Gate, as attested by the shipments *via* Richmond from New York. In addition to what has been denominated as the Chesapeake and Ohio railway system proper, the Northwestern system runs from Lexington, Ky., to Covington, Ky., (Cincinnati), 99 miles; from Cincinnati over the C. I., St. L. and C. line to Kankakee, 253 miles, connecting with the Illinois Central, 56 miles, to Chicago—making the comparative distances between Atlantic ports and principal Western railroad centres by the Chesapeake and Ohio system and its projected connections, and by other trunk lines, as follows:

MILES FROM PORT OF—	To Cincinnati.	To Louisville.	To St. Louis	To Memphis.	To Nashville.	To Columbus, O.	To Indianapolis.	To Chicago.
Richmond, *via* Ches. and Ohio....	573	643	913	1020	828	564	688	832
Baltimore, *via* Balt. and Ohio......	589	696	929	1073	881	513	705	839
Philadelphia, *via* Penn. railroad...	668	778	964	1155	963	548	736	823
New York, *via* Erie railway..........	861	988	1201	1365	1173	755	935	983
New York, *via* N. Y. Central........	883	940	1144	1393	1176	761	830	980
Boston, *via* N. Y. Central.............	941	998	1202	1426	1234	829	888	1038

The line runs in Virginia and West Virginia from Richmond *via* Gordonsville, Charlottesville and Staunton to the Ohio river. It drains the upland tobacco, corn and wheat sections of Eastern Virginia, the great granaries of "the great Valley," bisecting the vast coal basins of West Virginia, and pierces the very heart of some of the most extensive beds of iron and other ores in the whole southern country. The coal supply, contiguous to the road, is practically beyond computation, and the expense of mining is reduced to a minimum compared with the cost in many other fields. Shaft work, usually such a heavy charge, is unknown, except for air holes, which can be sunk for a trifling sum. The character of the coals are bituminous, and semi-bituminous viz: Cannel, splint, gas, and pure bituminous steam coals—the superior quality of which, for domestic use and the various mechanic arts for which they are severally adapted, having been well established. The iron ores comprise nearly all the varieties used in the manufacture of iron and steel Along the line of the road are also immense stretches of virgin forest, the timber consisting of oak, yellow poplar, black walnut, hickory, cherry, sycamore, pine, and other varieties in demand for manufacturing purposes. It has been proven by actual working, and is now not disputed, that iron can be manufactured from the ore along the Chesapeake and Ohio railway at a lower cost than in any other portion of the country—a fact that has already led to numerous plants being made by Northern and English capitalists, and created a valuable source of demand upon Richmond, as well as a source of supply for her manufactures. Near Charlottesville the road crosses the Virginia Midland from Danville to Alexandria; at Waynesboro', just west of the Blue Ridge, the Shenandoah Valley from Hagerstown, Maryland, to Roanoke, Virginia, on the Norfolk and Western railroad; and at Staunton the Valley railroad from Harper's Ferry to Lexington, Virginia, all of which traverse rich and populous sections of country. In a picturesque point of view the country from the eastern slope of the Blue Ridge to Huntington is nowhere excelled. Westward and south-westward from Huntington the line passes through Blue Grass country, and lays under tribute an immense grain and tobacco growing area. The wheat of this section is particularly suited to the needs of the large milling interest of the city, in the manufacture of the celebrated Richmond brands of flour which have held for nearly a century the chief place in the South American trade. By its northwestern connections, as shown in the comparative table of distances, it also reaches by short and direct route and low grades the great northwestern grain centres. The Newports News extension, though but recently completed, is the realization of the dream of years of those who have studied the interests of Richmond and Virginia. Here the system has immense wharves and warehouses, and owns a water front capable of accommodating any conceivable demand of shipping. The depth of water is sufficient to float the largest vessels. The line drains a country hitherto cut off from railroad communication with any point.

RICHMOND AND ALLEGHANY RAILROAD.

The Richmond and Alleghany railroad follows the line of the old James River and Kanawha canal—the initial link of Washington's favorite scheme for mingling the waters of the James and Ohio rivers—from Richmond through Scottsville, Columbia and Lynchburg, to Buchanan, thence to Williamson's, on the Chesapeake and Ohio railway, 230.31 miles, with branch line to

Balcony Falls, 174.50 miles west of Richmond, to Lexington, Rockbridge county, Virginia, 19.38 miles. It also has under lease the Henrico railroad, which connects with its main line a short distance above Richmond, and passes through the Henrico coal-fields to Hungary station on the Richmond, Fredericksburg and Potomac railroad. The total trackage finished and operated is 260.09 miles. The road was chartered February 27, 1879, and drains the beautiful James River Valley—the garden spot of Virginia—which, prior to its completion, was off the line of any railway. The agricultural districts contiguous to the road are unsurpassed for richness and variety of product by any section of the whole country, while the mineral deposits along the road, and demanding an outlet by it, are exceptionally extensive. In iron ores the James River Valley especially emphasises the statement of Wiley, that "Pennsylvania, rich as she is, is poor in iron ores compared with Virginia" Some years ago Professor Rogers, late Emeritus Professor in the Massachusetts Institute of Technology, published a most valuable and a standard series of reports on the Geological Formations of Virginia, in which the inexhaustible mineral wealth of the State was fully classified and demonstrated, but it has been left for John L. Campbell, A. M., LL. D., Professor of Geology and Mineralogy, at Washington and Lee University, to illustrate the preponderating mineral wealth of the James River Valley. Professor Campbell's explorations represent months of patient mental toil and physical exertion, and his opinions have been formed, as he states, without reference to the interests of any individual or company, but solely in the interests of science, and of the State of Virginia. He may be said to have literally investigated the mineral deposits accessible by the road, step by step The work was accomplished before the road was completed, and in his report Professor Campbell says:

"My leading purpose is to elucidate and enforce the following two or three fundamental facts: (1) The canal and its railway connection traverse every one of the *five great ore-bearing geological formations* of Virginia, and one of the finest limestone regions in America. (2) In these formations, or belts, we find in great abundance and of superior quality, *every variety* of ore that is profitably worked for iron anywhere in the world, with the exception of the carbónates, like the "clay iron-stones" and "black band" ores of England, which are impure carbonates found in the coal regions. (3) Other minerals, besides iron ores, that promise to become sources of revenue to the State as well as to the Company, abound in this valley."

This he does in the clearest and most satisfactory manner dividing the ores into five belts, giving assays of specimens from each belt, and showing that limestones hitherto employed so successfully for fluxing, are found in close proximity to all the deposits. Fuel is the only thing to be transported any distance in order to reduce these ores and that is accessible in any quantity, through the connection of the line at Williamson's with the Chesapeake and Ohio Railway. Besides this the Richmond and Alleghany is already projected to Pittsburg, Pa., through other extensive coal deposits. In addition to iron ores, there are near to the line or immediately upon it, kaolin, sand of a superior quality for making glass, the manganese and copper ores of Nelson and Amherst counties, the barytes of Botetourt and Rockbridge counties, the partially worked gold mines of Fluvanna, Buckingham and Appomattox, the granite quarries above Richmond, and the slate quarries of Buckingham. Since the road has been in operation there has been quite an influx of settlers to some of the counties through which it passes—which has made itself most perceptibly felt upon Richmond trade. Among the property acquired by the railroad company in the transfer of the franchises of the James River and Kanawha Canal Company were 6,800 feet of available dockage on the river front of the lower portion of the city, together with one of the most valuable water powers in the Union. The connection with the Norfolk and Western system at Lynchburg, is also a great acquisition to Richmond. This line runs through Liberty, Salem, the iron, lead and zinc formations, and the rich pasture lands and forests of southwestern Virginia, into East Tennessee, giving another great system to the West, and with the Chesapeake and Ohio, and the Alleghany connection with that road at Williamson's, an advantage in the matter of grades that is beyond dispute. This single item is of incalculable value and importance to Richmond. The grades of the Richmond and Alleghany between Lynchburg and Richmond average but four feet to the mile.

THE ATLANTIC COAST LINE.

The Atlantic Coast Line system (see map) is the second great trunk line connecting Richmond with the South. The total trackage from Richmond south controlled by the system is 566 miles, as follows: Richmond and Petersburg railroad, Richmond, Va., to Petersburg, Va., 25 miles; Petersburg railroad, Petersburg to Weldon, N. C., 65 miles; Wilmington and Weldon railroad and Tarboro' Branch, Weldon, N. C., to Wilmington, N. C., 182 miles; Wilmington, Columbia and Augusta railroad, Wilmington, N. C., to Columbia, S. C., 192 miles; Northeastern railroad, Florence, S. C., to Charleston, S. C., 102 miles. At Charleston the system connects with the Charleston and Savannah railroad, from Charleston, S. C., to Savannah, Ga., 115 miles; thence over the Savannah, Florida and Western railroad to Jacksonville, Fla., 172 miles. The line crosses the Norfolk and Western system at Petersburg, the Seaboard and Roanoke railroad at Weldon, and passes *via* Goldsboro', on the Richmond and Danville system, through the immense pine stretches of North Carolina and the lower cotton belts of South Carolina and Georgia. Through its cross lines and connections it must draw the entire traffic to the east in the three last named States; while to the west it drains the whole country between it and the Danville system not tributary to the latter. In the logic of trade and traffic these two systems must make Richmond their natural base of supply, and reciprocally the depot of concentration, for the shipment or distribution elsewhere, in manufactured or crude form, of their overplus of raw material. At Chester, Va., on the Richmond and Petersburg railroad, the system crosses the Brighthope railroad, extending from Bermuda Hundreds, on James river, to the Brighthope coal district, in Chesterfield county. The country along the line of the road depends altogether upon Richmond for its supplies. The lands in this region, having a triassic basis, are admirably adapted to the production of cigar ("Seed leaf") tobacco, when the production of that special type shall be added to those which have already made Virginia famous as a tobacco State.

RICHMOND, FREDERICKSBURG AND POTOMAC RAILROAD.

This is the great short line from Richmond *via* Fredericksburg to Quantico, on the Potomac river, 82 miles from Richmond, connecting at Quantico with the Pennsylvania system to Washington, 34 miles, thence to New York, Boston, and the New England manufacturing centres. It passes in Virginia through many of the important battle-fields of the late war, and connects at Richmond with the short line south and southwest for passenger traffic. By it our jobbers have the most direct and quickest route for obtaining, by fast freight and express, from the North what is not supplied by the Richmond manufactories. There are three through passenger trains over it each way daily, and it is one of the best equipped and safest roads in the Union. Over this line the tobacco manufacturers of Richmond receive the bulk of the famous leaf, known as the "Caroline Sun-cured," which leaf furnishes the stock for the finest grades of plug tobacco made in the world.

WATER COMMUNICATION.

The wharf frontage improved at Rocketts, the lower end of the city, is 3,000 feet on the north side, and 1,500 feet on the south side of James river. That of the Chesapeake and Ohio Railroad Company just below the city is 1,000 feet, add to this the 6,800 feet of dockage controlled by the Richmond and Alleghany Railroad Company, and we have a grand total of 12,300 feet. This wharfage capacity can be extended indefinitely. The depth of water in the dock is fourteen feet, sufficient to float the majority of coasting vessels. The depth in the river over the bar is eighteen feet. In this connection, however, it should be noted that Congress authorized a special commission of army engineer-officers to make a survey of the James river, with a view to the increase of its depth to twenty-four feet. They have made their report, and declare it entirely feasible. Such depth of water is desired not only for our export trade, but for the entrance of raw material by sail vessels for use in our manufactories. This work of improvement has been pushed forward with energy, each year showing a greater depth of water. The regular lines of steamers from Richmond, exclusive of the river line to Norfolk, are the Old Dominion for New York, the Powhatan for Baltimore, and the Clyde line for Philadelphia. From West Point, the Old Dominion for New York, the Boston and Providence for Boston, and the York River line for Baltimore. From Newports News the Brazilian and United States mail steamship line. In order to give a fair idea, however, of the facilities afforded Richmond, in the way of water transportation, we have recourse to the Report of the Harbor Master for the year 1881. Number of vessels arriving at Port of Richmond: steamers 560, capacity 490,000 tons; sailing vessels, 861, tonnage 205,000; class: barks, 48; brigs, 35; schooners, 778. This does not include river steamers, tug-boats or small sailing vessels.

CHAPTER III.

GENERAL MANUFACTURING EXHIBIT.

CAPITAL INVESTED, HANDS EMPLOYED, AGGREGATE SALES, SPECIAL ADVANTAGES, WATER AND STEAM POWER, LABOR SUPPLY, RAW MATERIAL AVAILABLE, FOSTERING AUXILIARIES.

The manufacturing labored, if possible, under greater disadvantages, after the war, than any other Richmond interest. Nevertheless, its progress has been most rapid and successful. Taking the statistics for 1881 as compiled for the annual trade edition of the Richmond *Dispatch*, we have the following showing as regards kinds of manufactories in operation, capital in business, and annual sales:

Kind of Manufactories.	Capital in Business.	Annual Sales.
Agricultural implements, machinery, &c.	$ 186,500	$ 510,000
Ale, beer and mineral waters	27,500	39,000
Bags and cotton bagging	60,000	94,980
Bakers	75,100	241,200
Bark and sumac	153,000	242,300
Barrels and hogsheads	32,840	461,800
Blacksmiths and wheelwrights	9,800	95,400
Blank-books, paper-boxes and paper-bags	115,000	395,700
Boots, shoes, leather, and leather goods	195,210	916,800
Boxes, cigar, tobacco and packing	164,000	338,400
Brand and stencil cutters	700	3,300
Bricks	105,000	160,000
Brooms, wood and willow-ware	142,500	400,250
Burial-caskets	5,000	15,000
Candy and confections	77,500	396,500
Carriages, wagons, carts, &c	122,425	201,450

TABLE—Continued.

Kind of Manufactories.	Capital in Business.	Annual Sales.
Carpenters and builders	$ 50,500	$ 324,900
Cigars and cigarettes	324,915	1,346,025
Coffee, spice and flavoring mills	48,000	235,000
Clothing, and merchant-tailors	203,300	490,500
Cotton factories	280,000	410,000
Drugs, medicines, meat-juice and bitters	298,200	982,300
Dyeing and bleaching	8,000	23,500
Earthen and stone-ware	5,500	12,000
Engraving on wood and lithographing	29,000	64,000
Fertilizers	690,000	1,150,000
Flour and corn-meal	1,331,500	3,148,661
Furniture, mattresses, &c.	111,000	306,000
Granite-works	395,000	301,500
Gunsmiths and sporting apparatus	12,100	20,500
Hair-workers	11,500	37,000
Iron and nail works, machine works, foundries, stove works, architectural iron works, tobacco fixtures, &c	1,642,000	5,337,590
Lubricators, oil and grease	28,000	82,000
Marble and stone works	23,000	74,000
Nets and seines	6,000	7,000
Newspapers and job printers	181,300	392,500
Paper mills	125,000	190,000
Picture frames and ornamental wood-work	67,000	176,500
Pork packing	115,000	1,300,000
Rectifiers	40,000	218,000
Saddles, harness and horse collars	73,350	182,600
Sash, blinds, doors, &c	112,000	449,900
Saw, wire and mill-fixture works	17,000	51,500
Slate works	40,000	50,000
Soap and candles	40,000	65,500
Sulphuric acid and sulphate of ammonia	20,000	10,000
Tanners	30,000	70,500
Tin-ware, gas-fittings and plumbing	140,975	446,700
Tobacco—chewing and smoking	2,831,000	9,071,000
Tobacco—stemmeries and reprizers	420,000	825,000
Trunks and valises	10,000	46,000
Type foundry	10,000	41,500
Underwear—ladies and gentlemen	78,500	351,000
Totals	$11,320,815	$32,802,756

The total number of manufactories was 675. Total number of hands permanently employed 17,648—an increase in operatives over the year 1880 of 716. The increase of annual sales over 1880 was $8,097,864, or about 33 per cent., and increase of capital invested $2,628,198. These figures do not include a number of minor establishments. That this, however, is only an earnest of Richmond's possibilities as a manufacturing centre, let us present *seriatim* a few points which must strike every practical mind.

FIRST—WATER POWER ADVANTAGES.

* From the three-mile lock, on the line of the Richmond and Alleghany railroad to tide-water, there is a fall of 84 feet. With the lowest flow of the river to be expected, in a long series of years, viz: 1,000 cubic feet per second, this fall produces 9,500 horse-power theoretically, of which 7,600 can be made available by the employment of the best turbine wheels. The total amount of this theoretical power, now appropriated and put to use by various manufactories in Richmond and Manchester, is 4,200; the remainder 5,300 horse-power theoretically, or 4,160 actual, can be readily and economically made available. From Bosher's Dam to tide-water is a fall of 116 feet, over which the above flow of the river would produce 13,500 theoretical horse-power, or 10,000 actual. The water shed of the James river above Richmond is about 8,000 square miles. The lowest flow given above is therefore a yield of 0.125 cubic feet per second from each square mile. The Connecticut river, with about the same water shed, yields at Holyoke, Massachusetts, about 0.30 cubic feet per second per square mile, as the lowest flow, and the Merrimac river at Lowell is relied upon for more than double this rate per square mile. A large part of this difference, however, is, of course, due to the different character of the water sheds, but still a large part to the fact that these two New England rivers, and especially the Merrimac, are used extensively for power along their entire length, and each little mill acts, to some extent, as a regulator. The James river with its thirteen large dams, and eleven minor ones, built by the James river and Kanawha

---

* These facts were expressly compiled for this publication by a competent hydrostatic engineer.

Terre

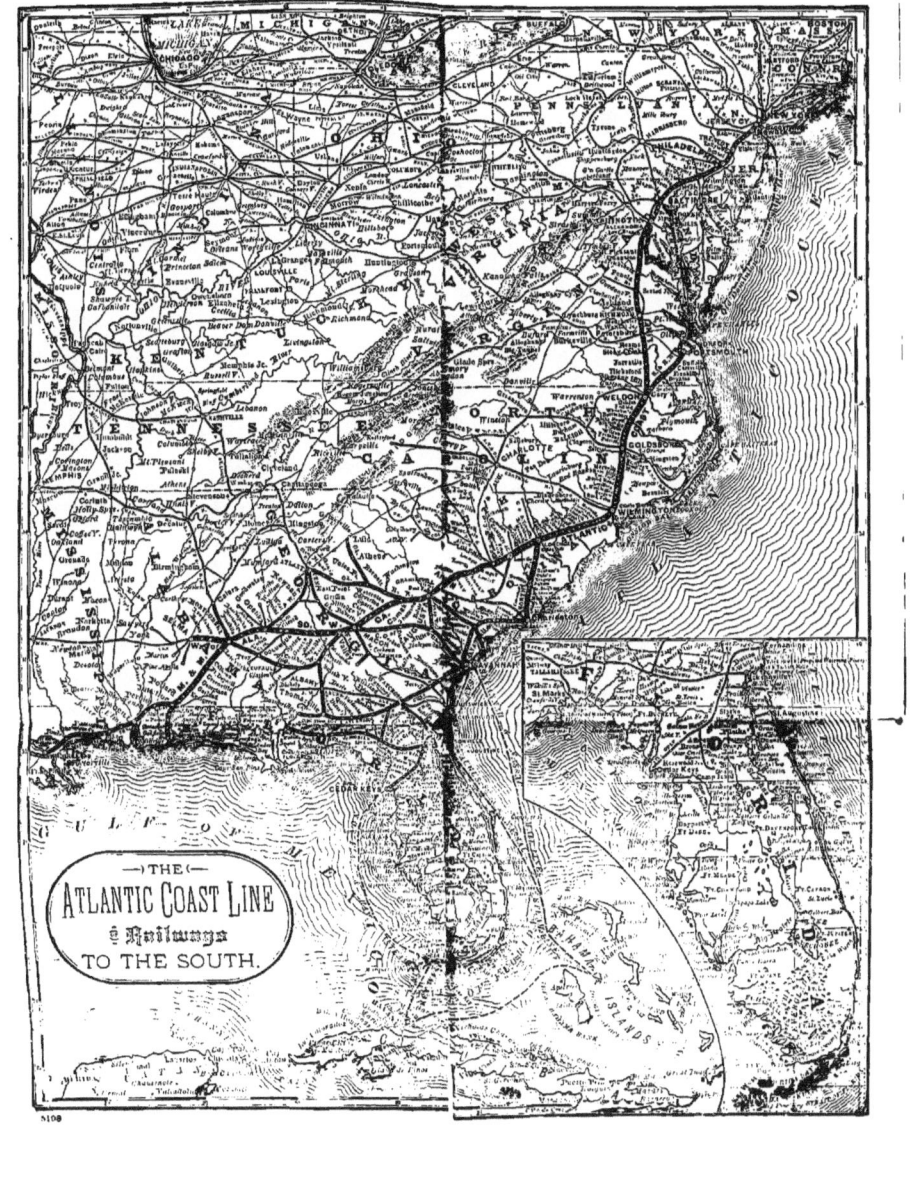

Canal Company, and the ten dams on the Rivanna river, one of its largest tributaries, possesses great facilities for the increase of the lowest flow, which, although not now available, could be readily made so. These dams form a series of ponds, with a total surface area of 291,200,000 square feet. If one foot of depth were available for storage, this would yield 168 cubic feet per second for a period of twenty days, to help out in the dry season. If two feet were available, the quantity would be doubled, or the same amount spread over twice as long a time. In addition to this, which can be immediately and cheaply taken advantage of, the natural growth of small industries along the Valley, which the mineral and agricultural wealth of the country must foster, will continually tend to average the yearly flow of the river. Again— the character of the upper water shed of the river, with its numerous tributaries, flowing long distances through immense furrows, between parallel ridges, now approaching so closely as to almost bar the passage of the stream, and at other points forming wide valleys, makes it possible, at warrantable expense, to form large basins for storage.

In view of all these considerations, it is a low estimate to say that the James river can be made to yield, as it can be put to use, a total of 20,000 effective horse-power over the Falls between Bosher's Dam and tide-water. The amount of power now put to use at Holyoke, Mass., which is rated as the largest developed water-power in the country, may be estimated as between 8,000 and 9,000 horse-power. The Hudson River Water-Power and Paper Manufacturing Company estimate their available power at 6,000 horse-power, and claim to be the second largest. By properly planning the improvements necessary to make the large reserve of power available—improvements which the south side of James river are admirably adapted to allow—the whole Falls plantation, opposite Rocketts, could be converted into a manufacturing plant—a plant virtually on the seaboard, and the centre of railroad facilities.

SECOND—STEAM-POWER FACILITIES.

It is only necessary to glance at the country through which the various railroad lines that centre at Richmond pass to see that steam-power can also be employed at the minimum cost. The steam coals of the various basins are, it has been practically demonstrated, of the best and most economical quality; easily mined and cheaply transported.

THIRD—LABOR SUPPLY.

The labor supply of Richmond is equal to any demand and of a character easily adapted to the requirements of most any industry. In fact nothing has more clearly and satisfactorily demonstrated the resources of our population—the white population particularly—than its accommodation to the exigencies of the new *regime*. The negro in the heavier work of rolling mills, and as a stevedore, &c., is a most valuable hand, while in the manufacture of plug tobacco he practically enjoys a labor monopoly. In temper he is tractable, and can be easily taught. The white artizan class has of late years absorbed elements from nearly every walk in life—disposition as well as necessity leading many to embrace mechanical pursuits, who under the old system in the South would not have had either the stimulus or the inclination to do so. The prejudice in favor of a profession is fast becoming a thing of the past. Many of the owners of manufacturing establishments have served their time during the last seventeen years. Prior to the war the employment of female operatives in manufacturing establishments was the exception—in fact there were few callings in which they could have been employed—even had it been customary or profitable. Now, however. the industrial element among white women and girls is very large and is constantly increasing, and daily new industries are being developed which are open to them In the manufacture of cotton goods paper, cigarettes, tobacco bags, paper bags, underwear, clothing, paper boxes, and in other light employments they are able to meet the most exacting demands for celerity and neatness of work. For the most part these operatives are reasonably well educated, are thoroughly reliable, and are not only contented but happy in their occupations. Moreover, they are naturally refined and art loving, a gift that could be utilized to great advantage in the manufacture of fine pottery, or any other industry requiring an art perception. It is a source of peculiar gratification to note in this connection the fact that our employers of female labor throw every safeguard possible around their employees, thus protecting them against temptations to which they are at many other manufacturing centres too often exposed.

FOURTH—RAW MATERIALS IN PART AVAILABLE FOR MANUFACTURING PURPOSES.

BY RICHMOND AND DANVILLE SYSTEM.—Wheat, corn, tobacco, cotton, kaolin, feldspar, mica, barytes, clays for building-brick and fire-brick, graphite, gold, iron and copper ores in great variety; ochre, granite, coal, limestone, quick-lime, lead, manganese, carbonate magnesia, soapstone, asbestos, hornblende, nickel, slate, sandstone, brownstone, buhrstone, marbles, white and variegated; glass sands, agate, jasper, silver, sulphur, turpentine, tar, rosin, asphalt, sumac, various minerals for ground paints; oak, pine, walnut, poplar, maple, willow, locust, plum, hickory, gum, dogwood, birch, cherry, persimmon, and some forty other varieties of wood of commercial value.

BY CHESAPEAKE AND OHIO SYSTEM.—Wheat, corn, wool, tobacco, coal, iron, gold ores, copper, and iron pyrites, lead, antimony, manganese, salt, kaolin, fire clay, hoop-poles, cement, limestone, sandstone, hides, staves, leather, lime, bark, pig-iron, plaster, sumac, petroleum, and numerous varieties of woods for cabinet and machinery purposes and building.

BY ATLANTIC COAST LINE.—Cotton, corn, wheat, sumac, rice, deer tongue, jute, tobacco, tar, pitch, rosin, turpentine, coal, sumac, lumber for building, and nearly all the woods available by the Richmond and Danville system.

BY RICHMOND AND ALLEGHANY RAILROAD.—Coal, copper, wool, oats, gold ores, limestone, cement, manganese, barytes, fire clay, kaolin, staves and hoop-poles, granite, leather, sumac, glass sand, hides, plaster, wheat, corn, tobacco, sandstone, mica, slate, and the woods found along the line of the Chesapeake and Ohio system.

BY NORFOLK AND WESTERN SYSTEM.—Through the Alleghany connection with this road there are available to Richmond, among other articles, corn, wheat, oats, iron, lead, zinc and copper ores, salt, plaster, hides, cattle, wool, cotton, and numerous commercial woods.

These lists only embrace leading and the more bulky articles. The materials used, in whole or part, for many industries—and which the statement of the general sub-division of Richmond manufactories shows are essential—are very numerous By water there is also available a large variety of raw material for the manufacture of fertilizers, wooden-ware, &c. A detailed exhibit from at least two of the railroad systems—the Richmond and Danville and Chesapeake and Ohio—is now in the Exhibition building at Boston.

FIFTH—FOSTERING AUXILIARIES.

Richmond, as the capital of the State, is the point for all State gatherings of any importance, and the scene of the meeting of many inter-State conventions. The historic interest attaching to it alone has made it very popular for such purposes. Further, it is the headquarters of the State Agricultural Society, which holds annual exhibitions near the city for the display not only of agricultural products and machinery, but all classes of machinery and manufactured goods These fairs bring together people from all parts of the country. The merchants from Virginia and the South avail themselves of the opportunity to replenish their stocks. The subject of rebuilding the Mechanics' Institute, destroyed by fire, is being agitated by the public-spirited business men, and it is only a question of a short time when the matter will take practical shape. Another organization which promises to exercise a decided influence in the advancement of the industrial arts is the Richmond Art Association, now in its sixth year. Already it has opened a new field for the employment of ladies, in stimulating the work of porcelain decoration.

SIXTH—PRESENT AND FUTURE DEMANDS.

There is now a pressing call for every class of article of Richmond manufacture, but this is little more than the suggestion of what may be reasonably expected for the future. The west and northwest are being rapidly filled up, and the tide of immigration must inevitably seek the fruitful fields of the South. In fact it has already turned in this direction. Whether this new population engage in agriculture—as a large percentage of it will—in mining, or in the ruder manufacturing pursuits, there is virtually no end to the demand that must be created for the production of skilled labor in the mechanic arts. The manifest destiny of the southern and southwestern country, still in the infancy of its development in many respects, reached by the railroad lines diverging from Richmond, is such as will compel the use of an interminable variety of manufactured articles, for labor-saving, comfort and convenience. With Richmond nearly two hundred miles nearer the supply of raw material, and the same distance nearer the fields of demand—practically four hundred miles saved as a question of freights—than any northern manufacturing centre, and with the other advantages heretofore set forth, it would be against the natural order of things if it should fail to influence this entire trade.

CHAPTER IV.

MANUFACTURES IN DETAIL.

THE BANKING BASIS—THE COAL MOVEMENT—THE IRON INTEREST—MILLING—A COMPREHENSIVE RANGE OF INDUSTRIES.

It has been shown that Richmond is the concentering point of a number of railroad lines—three of which, at least, constitute great trunk systems, opening up to it a territory unsurpassed in richness and variety of natural resources. That this territory can fail of development, to its fullest, is contrary to the law of capital and of progress. To the south, southwest, and west, the attractions of climate and soil, are the prophecy of a teeming population, which will require a basis of distribution of the largest capacity. It is only necessary to glance at the map, to be impressed not only with the distance saved as before stated, but the time as well, from this territory in favor of Richmond as against the more northern markets. It is only necessary to bear in mind the city's connections by rail and by water with the North, to be convinced of the ability of our business men to place in the depots and on the wharves, at bottom freight rates, all the necessary articles that may be demanded by the Southern trade, which are not at present manufactured in the city. The Richmond merchants in buying North, buy on an equality with the Northern jobbers, and the superadded freight rates from Richmond to the northern points of supply count as nothing to the consumer or merchant South, by reason of the greatly reduced cost of doing business in Richmond. In fact, the trade south has on all northern articles bought in Richmond, the difference in the cost of transportation between Richmond and the North, in its favor, to say nothing of what may be conceded, through the decreased expense of handling alluded to; while on articles of Richmond manufacture still greater advantages are a natural sequence. These facts, it must be apparent to every clear-headed business man, claim the consideration, not only of the southern buyer, but of capital seeking investment. It has also been demonstrated that Richmond possesses every other advantage regarded by capitalists as essential to the building up of a great city, and a great centre of supply and distribution—such as water power, healthy location, security in time of war, tractable labor, &c.,— but in presenting the most forcible and conclusive argument in support of the claims advanced we have again to revert to "what has been done by the people with the limited means at their disposal and the drawbacks that beset them." This it is true has been outlined in general terms, but in order to convey its full significance, it is competent to show the status of the various interests more in detail

FINANCE AND BANKING.

In April, 1865, Richmond as a corporation was bankrupt. One-half of the taxable realty had been swept away, and the people were without a currency—without even the means of barter. To day City bonds are above par—8's 128, 6's 112⅞, 5's 103 bid—and are counted as among the best securities in the market. The banks of the city are eleven in number—four of them National banks. The total banking capital is $2,200,000, with a surplus of $555,000. Besides, all the local insurance companies are lenders of money, and much is secured through re-discounts by banks North. During the panic of 1873 the solidity of these institutions was most satisfactorily demonstrated in that they weathered the storm, when banks were failing all around them. There is also a regular stock board in the city, which is most conservatively conducted—no "wild cat" securities of any sort being allowed upon the call. The members are all brokers of well known integrity. The local insurance companies are all safe institutions.

THE COAL MOVEMENT.

The coal movement is a most important factor in its relations to the manufacturing interests of Richmond. The supply is obtained over five lines of transportation, and from four fields, the West Virginia, the Midlothian, the Bright Hope, and the Henrico mines. The three latter are within a few miles of the city. For steaming, heating, puddling and smelting, and all other purposes for which coals can be used, they are held to be as valuable and economical as any coals mined anywhere in America, and the deposits are as yet but partially developed. It is estimated that in the immediate neighborhood of Richmond there is enough coal to meet the demand of hundreds of years. As an article of shipment it also occupies a prominent place in the trade of Richmond. During the year 1881, there were shipped from the Chesapeake and Ohio wharves alone 213,907 tons.

IRON-WORKS AND MACHINE-SHOPS.

The iron interest has made steady and successful progress in all departments for a series of years. The ore beds of Virginia are in such close proximity to coal and fluxing supplies, labor is so plentiful and transportation so convenient, that pig-iron for conversion into castings, wrought iron and steel, and forged iron, can be placed in the mills, shops and foundries at bottom figures. There are now over 4,000 men engaged in the several iron-working establishments in Richmond, and their productions represent nearly every article for which iron can be utilized. The amount of sales of this interest for 1881, was $5,337,590.

RAILROAD MATERIALS AND WROUGHT IRON SPECIALTIES.—Rails, spikes, fish-bars, bolts, freight cars, car wheels, axles, bridge iron, bridge bolts, railroad chairs. In addition to this, ground has been broken and shops are in process of erection for the building of freight and passenger locomotives and cars on an extensive scale, and the city does a large jobbing trade in locomotive head-lights, steam-cocks and gauges, lanterns, brasses and railroad supplies generally. This business has been rendered necessary and lucrative by the railroad interests centering at Richmond. In the establishments *manufacturing* the railroad material indicated, are also turned out bar-iron for general use, horse and mule shoes, nails, gratings, nuts and screws in great variety. The nail industry is the largest of any city in the South, and the mills are now greatly increasing their capacity.

ENGINE BUILDING.—The engine builders were, during last year, and are now, pressed to the utmost building capacity of their shops. During 1881, there were over 600 engines turned out in Richmond, a single concern shipping, during the busy season, an average of two engines a day. Among the specialties of the engine and machine shops, are portable engines, stationary engines, agricultural engines, locomotive boilers, plain cylinder, return tubular, return flue, and upright boilers, smoke-stacks, tanks and general boiler work, pumps and fittings for engines and boilers, steam fire-engines, mill machinery, hydraulic presses and pumps, shafting and pulleys, and saw-mills. The greater part of the engines manufactured are sold south and southwest.

CASTINGS.—In this department the stove business deserves a prominent place, Richmond supplying an immense trade south, west and southwest. We also mention turbine water wheels, mill gearing, plow points, verandas and railings. ornamental iron work, piping, and an endless number of smaller articles ; in fact it is unnecessary to go out of Richmond for any piece of casting.

MISCELLANEOUS.—Tobacconists' fixtures,—such as presses, shapes, pumps, tobacco knives, steam drying apparatus—saws, files, edge tools, fire grates and builders' materials

TOBACCO MACHINERY.

Besides the "tobacconists' fixtures," mentioned under the general head of "Iron Works and Machine Shops," the manufacture of "Tobacco Machinery" merits a distinct classification, as follows :—Elevators, leaf tobacco trucks, lump boxes, tobacco box groovers, flattening mills, blocks, billets, cutters for smoking tobacco bags, pot or finishing mills, power cutters, smoking tobacco cutters, tobacco stem-grinders, tobacco fans, lump machines, and granulators.

AGRICULTURAL IMPLEMENTS AND MACHINERY.

The manufacture of agricultural implements is hardly second to any business of the city, in the different implements manufactured, and in adding to the general business revenue. In considering this interest it should be noticed that the woods used are all right at the doors of the city. The list is too numerous to detail, but we give the leading articles, exclusive of agricultural engines :—threshing machines, horse powers, plows, harrows, corn planters, separators, cultivators, fertilizer distributers, horse rakes, gleaners, garden and field rollers, grindstone fixtures, cider mills, hand and power corn shellers, road scrapers, peanut pickers, shellers and separators, barrows, sausage machines and stuffers, gardening tools, straw and feed cutters, lifts, suction pumps and well fixtures, farm carts and wagons, and cotton presses. Agencies are established in Richmond for all the patent agricultural machines of recognized value, as well as for such domestic labor-saving machinery as are not manufactured in the city.

THE MILLING INTEREST.

The capacity of the Richmond flour mills, with the improved processes, is about 4,000 barrels of flour daily, and the Richmond brands have always held first rank in the South American market—in fact, as before noted, their superiority has been conceded from the first decade of the present century. Prior to the late civil war, the flour trade was a double source of revenue. A regular line of barks sailed between Richmond and the South American ports—carrying out flour, and returning laden with Brazilian coffees, and West Indian sugars and molasses, thus making the city one of the largest markets for these articles in the Union. The interruption of the war of course weaned much of this trade from us, but it has been gradually reviving, and, now that our railroad connections are so complete, it is confidently predicted that we will again become large direct importers. The statistics of the trade of Richmond with Brazil for the year 1881 show: value of coffee imported, $59,230; value of flour exported, $1,650,622; number of barrels of flour exported, 223,496. In addition to this there were also shipped to Brazil from West Point (port of Richmond), 76,777 barrels—making a grand total of 300,273. Number of vessels engaged in the trade, seventy-five sailing vessels, and nine steamships—total, eighty-six; the mills also produce a good deal of fine family flour for home trade, together with large quantities of meal—the greater proportion of which latter article is shipped to the south. Nearly all, if not all, of the wheat ground for the Brazilian market is from Virginia or Western States in the same parallel of latitude.

THE FLOUR AND GRAIN TRADE.

The flour and grain trade of Richmond, independent of what is known and termed the "milling interest," has received an immense impulse in late years, and the city is fast becoming one of the most prominent grain markets on the Atlantic coast. Flour is received for distribution, not only from the Virginia mills, but from the west, in large quantities, and the grain supply is drawn over three lines of road, reaching the west and northwest. During the year a grain elevator has been erected near the Chesapeake and Ohio railway depot, and from the first month of its completion has been pressed to its full capacity—over 450,000 bushels. To facilitate transactions in grain there is a regular "Corn and Flour Exchange." The overplus above mill consumption is shipped north and south or exported. Richmond enjoys a fine trade in wheat with both Spain and Portugal.

THE TOBACCO INTEREST.

By reason of seniority as a Virginia staple, and the amount of manipulation it requires from first to last, tobacco should probably be placed first on the list of Richmond industries. It has in time been the source of more large fortunes, and the cause of more legislation, than anything produced in this State. During the year 1881, the total tax paid the government, on tobacco, cigars and cigarettes, was $2,282,239.53. Number of hands employed on plug and smoking tobacco, 4,821; on cigars and cigarettes, 775; in stemming and re prizing, 579; total, 6,175. Amount of tobacco manufactured, 17,500,000 pounds. The total amount of internal revenue paid the government by the Richmond district from the close of the war to June 30, 1882, was $37,612,601.

LEAF TOBACCO.—Most of the leaf tobacco is sold by certified sample of inspectors, at auction on the Tobacco Exchange. The leaf tobacco year ends October 30th, but as a basis for calculation we give the statistics from October, 1880, to December 1, 1881, as far as they could be gathered:

Inspections.—From October, 1880, to October, 1881, 30,921 hogsheads, 5,084 tierces; from October, 1881, to December 1, 1881, 4,184 hogsheads, 333 tierces. Total, 35,105 hogsheads and 5,417 tierces.

Deliveries.—From October, 1880, to October, 1881, 32,615 hogsheads, 4,963 tierces; from October, 1881, to December 1,

1881, 5,003 hogsheads 450 tierces. Total, 37,618 hogsheads and 5,413 tierces.

Foreign Shipments Direct.—From October, 1881, to December 1, 1881, 867 hogsheads, 73 tierces.

Coastwise Shipments.—From October, 1881, to December 1, 1881, 1,242 hogsheads, 176 tierces.

Stock on Hand.—December 1, 1881: Inspected, 10,011 hogsheads, 314 tierces; uninspected, 755 hogsheads, 21 tierces. Total, 10,766 hogsheads and 335 tierces.

Loose Tobacco Receipts—From October, 1880, to October, 1881, 2,823,770 pounds; from October, 1880, to December 1, 1880, 53,510 pounds; from October, 1881, to December 1, 1881, 332,405. Excess for 1881, 278,895 pounds.

Between private individuals and the buyers for foreign governments, most of the stemmed and re-prized tobaccos are exported.

PLUG AND SMOKING TOBACCO.—This branch of the tobacco industry, of course, employs the largest number of hands and the largest amount of capital. The tobaccos used are Virginia, North Carolina and Western, and the trade extends all over the world. The Western, Southern and Australian trade is particularly heavy. In the commoner grades of tobacco nearly any sound leaf can be worked up, whether Virginia, North Carolina or Western; but tobaccos from certain sections of Virginia and North Carolina, are used almost exclusively in the highest grades, and Richmond brands, by reason of our proximity to the source of supply, enjoy a position of the first importance. The manufactured tobacco exported in 1881 was 3,566,698½ pounds. The total number of tobacco factories in 1881 was 55. This is exclusive of stemmeries, reprizing establishments, and cigarette and cigar factories.

CIGARS AND CIGARETTES.—Cigars are manufactured largely for the Southern and Western trade, and some few for export. The tobaccos used are principally Connecticut, Havana and Pennsylvania, which are bought in large quantities. The brands stand high, both at home and in the South, and the trade is rapidly increasing. The Richmond cigar-makers have fully demonstrated, as the demand upon them shows, that they can in every way compete with northern markets. The climate of Richmond is especially well adapted to the manipulation of cigar tobaccos. The manufacture of cigarettes is a comparatively new industry in

Richmond, but one that has grown beyond all precedent, as the following comparative table of the productions of the last seven years will show:

Date.	No. of Cigarettes.
1875	3,116,000
1876	13,887,000
1877	17,146,800
1878	19,293,000
1879	32,570,000
1880	52,259,440
1881	65,000,000

Of the total number manufactured in 1881, 24,154,000 were exported. The tobaccos worked up are the bright, aromatic smokers of southern Virginia and northern and western North Carolina, which, owing to the small percentage of nicotine and nitrates they contain, gives the Richmond cigarette the preference in all markets where pure tobaccos are appreciated. The bulk of the cigarettes used in the London clubs are made in Richmond. In rolling the cigarettes, labeling them, and putting them in packages, white girls are employed exclusively.

SUMAC AND BARK.

Sumac and bark mills may also be classed as recent features of Richmond industry. The gathering of sumac gives employment to a great number of the poorer classes in the country, and the ground article stands high in the Northern market. Bark for tanning and other purposes is accessible on all the railroads.

LEATHER, LEATHER FINDINGS, HARNESS, &c.

Tanning is carried on in the city quite extensively, and in leather, leather findings, harness, &c., the business is steadily increasing. It would surprise many of our own citizens to know how many hands are engaged in this business and the amount of improved machinery employed. Richmond harness and saddle work enjoys a reputation in the South second to that of no city in the country for excellence in quality and reasonable prices. All classes of the best work are made, and the demand is constant. The wholesale manufacture of shoes is also rapidly increasing, the capacity of the various factories being estimated at 2,500 pairs per day.

CARRIAGES, WAGONS, &c.

Richmond manufactures the best quality of carriages, wagons, carts and vehicles generally. The number of hands engaged in this industry including blacksmiths and wheelwrights is over 500. And the wood and iron findings are to hand, and enable the trade to confidently enter the field of competition for all reliable work. In the last few years the success of the business has justified a decided expansion in manufacturing facilities.

FURNITURE.

The furniture trade is assuming most important proportions, and our cabinet makers are manufacturing every grade of furniture from the finest to the most ordinary. Nearly every kind of wood now used in this industry is easily available to Richmond, even to the finest necessary for inlaid work. The woods in the railway displays at the Boston Exhibition will show the range. Richmond furniture is not only shipped south and west, but is sent abroad.

COOPERING AND BOX-MAKING.

The demand from the Richmond mills, the pork-packing establishments, the nail factories, the tobacco and cigar factories and jobbers, alone makes these industries count as a large factor in the city's manufactures. Hoop-poles and staves for coopering, and lumber for the box factories, form a large item of transportation over all the railroads. The demand for such productions also extends outside of the city.

SASH, BLINDS AND DOORS.

In the sash, blind and door factories, about two hundred hands are employed, and the trade extends as far south as Georgia. All classes of fine and medium goods are produced. The material reaches Richmond over all the lines of railroad, to be sent back in manufactured form. Fine mouldings and stair-work are a specialty with some of the factories.

COTTON FACTORIES.

The cotton factories employ about 400 hands, mostly women, and the industry is annually becoming more important, owing to the accessibility of raw material. Cotton is now one of the chief articles of transportation over the southern roads, and the city is taking position as a cotton market. A feature of the trade is the barter of fertilizers for cotton. In the cotton factories water-power is used exclusively. The materials turned out are cotton cloths and yarns, and the coarser fabrics, but there is every promise of the manufacture of prints in the near future. The woolen mill interest has not revived in Richmond since the war, but there is the best sort of opening, not only for the manufacture of woolen cloths, but such specialties as hosiery, &c. The city has a large trade in wool, drawing it from every direction, but especially from Piedmont and Southwestern Virginia, where particular attention is given to sheep-breeding, and the female labor is plentiful and well adapted for such an enterprise.

EARTHEN AND STONE-WARE.

Potters' clay of the best quality is abundant in the vicinity of Richmond, and has stimulated a profitable business in earthen ware; and the manufacture of fine china, &c., is only a question of a short time. In fact, a joint stock company for the manufacture of porcelain ware was formed last year, and a factory with all the improved machinery erected. This building was burned last spring, however, just as operations were about to be commenced. All the material for the finest classes of this ware, such as kaolin, flint and feldspar, is found in abundance in various portions of the State, and at other points easily accessible from Richmond. One immense bed of kaolin, of exceptional rare quality, is located only eight miles from the city, immediately on the line of the Richmond and Danville railroad, and goods manufactured entirely from Virginia material have been proven equal to any made in the United States. As before intimated, decorative art has received a great impetus lately, and the skilled labor for this department of porcelain manufacture is already at hand and anxious for employment.

BAGS AND BAGGING.

The wheat, flour, grain, smoking tobacco, and cotton trade makes this interest a necessity, which capital has not been slow to take advantage of. The manufacture of bags for flour for home consumption, and of smoking tobacco bags, is another interest nearly monopolized by women. The material for the manufacture of gunny bags is imported from India, but efforts are being made to raise it in Eastern North Carolina, with every prospect of success.

PORK PACKING.

Pork packing for the southern trade is carried on extensively, the meat being bought in bulk and on the hoof not only from Virginia, but from the great western centres. It is distributed to the extreme limits of southern railroad connections. The manufacture of sausage for the southern trade is an especially large interest.

CLOTHING AND UNDERWEAR.

In clothing and underwear Richmond is also able to compete with the northern manufacturing centres, buying what material not manufactured at home to the best advantage, and utilizing female labor. The shirt factories here turn out as fine work as can be produced anywhere, and many of the finer cloths for suitings are imported directly.

WOODEN-WARE, BROOMS AND WILLOW-WARE.

These industries employ as many as 200 hands, many of them skilled, and for the production of all the articles embraced under this heading the material is not only plentiful but most convenient. Among the articles manufactured of cedar are tubs of all sizes, pails, cans, field cans, staff churns, cylinder churns, well and horse buckets, and ice-pails, measures and keelers, the finish and thoroughness of work on which is not excelled anywhere, as the showing at the Exhibition will demonstrate. The lumber is brought for the most part from the great swamps of Virginia and North Carolina. In the wooden-ware business there is a fine opening for the investment of capital, in the manufacture of the smaller articles, such as spools, trays, spoons, trenchers, rolling-pins, clothes-pins, &c.

PAPER, BLANK BOOKS, PAPER BOXES, AND PAPER BAGS.

The paper mills turn out all grades of news, book and wrapping papers and paper twines—a large quantity of the wrapping paper being consumed in the manufacture of paper bags. In bookbinding and blank-book making, Richmond establishments cannot be excelled, either in low prices or good work. The manufacture of paper boxes is a prominent and increasing industry, and all the establishments are worked to their full capacity. Among the articles manufactured we mention smoking tobacco boxes, pill boxes in endless variety, powder boxes, confectioners' boxes and toilet boxes. These latter are of every design, and have given Richmond a reputation all over the country. In neatness of work, beauty of finish and general ornamentation they are not excelled by the finest French products. This industry gives employment to about 600 hands, most of them women and girls.

GRANITE AND MARBLE CUTTING.

Granite and marble cutting is a lucrative occupation in the items of preparing building material and in monumental work for home trade, but this is a small part of the industry. Richmond granite is known and in demand all over the country for street paving, and some of the finest work on several of the public buildings at Washington was executed here. The supply is practically inexhaustible, and for toughness and power of resistance to the action of fire and the weather it has no superior. The Richmond custom-house, which is built of this granite, was, at the great fire of the evacuation of the city by the Confederate troops, the centre of the "burnt district," and suffered no damage. Marble of a superior quality is, as before indicated, found on the line of several of the railroads leading into the city. Some of the varieties are beautifully adapted for the manufacture of soda fountains, mantels and furniture tops.

WOOD ENGRAVING, LITHOGRAPHING AND PRINTING.

These kindred occupations give employment to over 300 hands, exclusive of the printers engaged on newspaper work. One of the greatest sources of revenue to all of them is the demand for labels for tobacco boxes, cigar boxes, general ornamentation for fancy paper boxes, and railroad work, though the finest work is also turned out in the way of check and draft books, bonds, stocks, show cards, &c.

CARPENTERING AND BUILDING.

The number of men engaged in this business may be fairly estimated at 1,000, and the building operations going on at present give them all employment. The Richmond builders are a superior class of men, and trouble between them and their employees rarely, if ever, occurs. In truth, it may be said that nowhere is community of interest between employer and employee in all industries more generally recognized than in Richmond. Distinct from carpentering and building are the industries of slating, tinning and plumbing, in which about 350 hands are employed.

BRICK MAKING.

The clays about Richmond are of a superior quality for brick making, and the industry is a source of revenue for a large element of population.

SOAP AND CANDLES.

The Richmond factories turn out the best qualities of laundry and toilet soap in great variety, which, with their candle production, find a ready market at home, south and west.

RECTIFIERS.

This business involves a large amount of capital, and supplies a very large territory in the South. The spirits employed are chiefly from the Valley of Virginia and the West.

CANNED GOODS.

The adaptability of the country circumjacent to Richmond to the raising of all sorts of fruits and vegetables, has made the canning industry one of very considerable magnitude. A special feature of the canneries in and around Richmond is that the materials are either raised especially for the purpose, on the farms of the proprietors, or are the *overplus*, never the *refuse* of the market-garden production. The area under cultivation directly attached to the canneries, is about 1,500 acres. During the busy season about 700 hands are employed, and the total packing capacity of the industry is 70,000 cases of 25 cans each. A large quantity of the goods put up is exported, and there is no reason why the canning business should not be greatly increased.

CANDY AND CONFECTIONERY AND BAKING.

The candy factories do a thriving business in both plain and fancy candies. Even before the war our candies had a reputation in the country accessible to Richmond, which reputation has been more than sustained in late years. The baking of cakes and fancy crackers for shipment is also an important item. The business gives employment to over 200 hands; and the facilities of our flour market give it advantages that must be evident to buyers.

FERTILIZERS.

The means of distribution for such goods, especially southward, being so exceptionally good at Richmond, induced the erection here of not less than five factories for the preparation of chemical manures, and they all do a large business. Their trade covers six States and is continually expanding. Richmond has two acid chambers and one factory for the production of sulphate of ammonia, erected during the past two years. With the ability to secure the bulk of the raw material used by sail-ship, no point can produce such goods to greater advantage, certainly, as stated, for the very large consuming region south of us.

LUBRICATORS, AXLE GREASE, &c.

The railroad interest and machine shops of the city have fostered a great expansion in the manufacture of these articles, and year by year both the capital and number of hands engaged in the business have steadily increased. The overplus above home consumption is large, but finds ready sale.

TIN-WARE.

The manufacture of tin-ware is a specialty with a number of establishments, and the articles turned out embrace everything for which tin can be used. The large negro population in the South creates a good demand for tin utensils alone.

COFFEE AND SPICE MILLS.

The coffee and spice and flavoring mills manufacture full lines of all articles known to the trade as belonging under this head.

TRUNKS AND VALISES.

The manufacture of trunks and valises is a comparative new industry, but the results have fully justified the investment of capital in this direction.

SULPHURIC ACID, MEAT JUICE, &c.

The production of sulphuric acid, meat juice, bitters, and proprietary articles of various kinds, is an important consideration, both in the matter of capital and labor employed.

TYPE AND ELECTROTYPING.

The making of type and electrotypes is a successful and increasing business, and complete outfits can be supplied for the largest job, book and newspaper establishments.

MISCELLANEOUS.

Under the head of "Miscellaneous" we include a large variety of industries; among them gun-smithing, hair-working, net and seine making, brand cutting, dyeing and bleaching, ale, beer and mineral water bottling, scroll sawing, &c., which afford support to a large number of people. Every day new enterprises are springing up, and it is safe to say that there are hidden away from general observation hundreds of little shops not included in the table of manufactories given elsewhere, the aggregate of whose production is far from trifling.

SHIP BUILDING, &c.

In closing this chapter, there are two other points we deem especially worthy of consideration: 1st. The war demonstrated that Richmond was impregnable in time of war, and it is a fact that nearly all cities of any size in the world are inland. 2d. While our capitalists are already large owners in sailing vessels, with sufficient depth of water—which, it is beyond question, can be obtained—there is no reason why the city should not become a most desirable place for ship building. Operatives can work the year round with comfort, and all the materials needed for such an enterprise are readily available. The real estate business is in the hands of a superior class of men, and capitalists wishing to invest will be afforded every accommodation in examining such property as may be on the market.

CHAPTER V.

THE JOBBING TRADE.

HOW IT HAS BEEN BUILT UP—RICHMOND THE CLOSEST, CHEAPEST, AND MOST NATURAL MARKET FOR THE SOUTH—LIST OF JOBBING ENTERPRISES—SOME POTENT REASONS WHY THE TRADE WILL CONTINUE TO INCREASE.

The jobbing trade—the principal distributing channel of all manufactures and commerce—has, in attaining its present proportions, had multitudinous difficulties to overcome, but has finally secured for Richmond a name as a base of supply second to that of no city on the Atlantic Seaboard. The accomplishment of such a result is not only indicative of the energy, enterprise and public spirit of our merchants, but evidence *per se* of the city's natural advantages. At the close of the war Richmond had, we reiterate, everything to contend with. The South was drained, and it was compelled to have supplies. The city had neither the capital nor transportation facilities to furnish them. The northern markets were not slow to appreciate their opportunity, and before Richmond had regained the local trade enjoyed prior to the war, they had virtually occupied the whole Southern field. The lines of transportation naturally discriminated in their favor, and their ability to give better accommodations was a theory, if not a fact, that militated against any representation that Richmond could make, even in the territory immediately accessible. Nevertheless, step by step, the Richmond salesmen followed the extension of the railroad lines, slowly but steadily introducing their samples, until not only the people, but the railroad corporations, alive to self-interest, began to take cognizance of their claims. It was a fact apparent, that wherever Richmond got a foot-hold it was able to remain; and when once the tide of trade set in this direction, the flow was continuous and increasing. How far the railroads were impressed with this is told by the most cursory examination of the maps accompanying this publication. Richmond, with its lines of local railway, extending south only to Greensboro, N. C., 186 miles, and west to Covington,

Va., 205 miles, is a thing of the past, and in its stead we have Richmond, the focus of a system, or systems, of transportation, that, by reason of no diverting points south of us, drains more area of country, and richer country at that, than any city in the Union. The jobbing trade was literally nothing to begin with. To-day we know of houses which, starting on a borrowed capital of a few thousand dollars, do a business of nearly a half million dollars annually. And it is no idle boast that we can and do compete with any city, north or south, in supplying any line of goods for the consumer or merchant.

THE REASONS.

This latter assertion is justified by every fact and argument we have heretofore advanced in advocacy of Richmond's claims as a manufacturing centre. But in order to enforce their relations to the specialty under consideration let us briefly re-state some of them in connection with other points that must strike the observer's mind:

First. Richmond is nearly two hundred miles nearer the southern, western and southwestern fields of demand than any city north of it, and from the west particularly is approached by easier grades than any other Atlantic port.

Second. A large line of goods are manufactured in Richmond and our jobbers can buy what is not manufactured here on exactly the same terms that the Northern jobbers can.

Third. The cost of doing business in Richmond is, by reason of the reduced cost of living so much below northern cities that our jobbers are enabled to ignore the difference in freights between Richmond and the Northern trade centres, which difference the Southern merchant would have to pay in buying North.

Fourth. Richmond can give shipments twelve hours in advance, and deliver goods twenty-four hours earlier from time of shipment than any Northern city, with much lower freight rates on account of distance.

Fifth. Tickets from any point South to Richmond and return, are cheaper than to any northern trade centre and return—a consideration of some importance to the merchant buying directly from the house in preference to buying from the salesman.

Sixth. Richmond has every advantage of competition in freights from western cities by rail, and from eastern cities by both rail and water, and has a fair and just tariff to the South, not inimical to the city.

Seventh. Situated at the head of tidewater where vessels drawing eighteen feet of water can come to the wharves, with rail connections to

West Point and Newports News (ports of Richmond), where the depth of water is sufficient for the largest vessels, the city has every facility for its import and export trade.

PASSENGER TRAFFIC.

That these conditions are favorable to a continued increase of the jobbing trade does not admit of argument, much less of dispute. The reasoning they convey in their bearing upon the future can bring us to but one conclusion; yet there are other reasons equally as potent in the premises, one of which is especially worthy of consideration. Richmond is on the great highway of passenger traffic from all points South to the North, and this service is as cheap and comfortable, as quick and as varied, as over any other line, having the advantage of both rail and water connection from here to the North. The northern bound traveller has the choice of the Richmond, Fredericksburg and Potomac line, the fast mail, passenger and express line north, or any of the several boat lines. Tickets *via* Richmond are sold at all stations and ticket offices at the same prices as *via* any other route. This is and must remain the popular route; and to the Southern merchant common sense and common business principles would dictate a trial of the Richmond market, before going further north, in order that he may institute a comparison of prices, freight rates, quantity of stock carried in his line, and post himself regarding such other matters as influence trade. If he goes direct to some northern point he loses the benefit of competition, not knowing the prices and advantages of Richmond. Such trial is all the Richmond merchants have ever asked in the past, or will ask in the future, to vindicate their assertion that this is the best, cheapest, closest, and most natural market for the southern trade. The test has been applied with the opening of every new feeder to the southern and southwestern railroad systems and with invariable success.

CLASSIFICATION.

The jobbing trade of Richmond now covers four entire States, and extends into portions of four others. A list of the articles sold by the jobbing houses would be interminable, but we mention the leading trade classifications with the simple assurance that all of the lines are complete:

AGRICULTURAL IMPLEMENTS—Agencies for all the leading man-

RICHMOND, VIRGINIA.

ufactories. BAKERS AND CONFECTIONERS. BOOKSELLERS AND STATIONERS. BOOT AND SHOE DEALERS—Handling every variety of home-made work and the products of all the leading New England manufactories. BOOT AND SHOE FINDINGS. BUILDERS' HARDWARE. CABINET-MAKERS' WARES. CANNED GOODS. CARPETS AND OIL CLOTHS. CATTLE. CHINA, GLASS AND CROCKERY-WARE—Including bric-a-brac. CIGARS—Domestic and imported. CLOTHING. COAL AND WOOD. COTTON—Raw. COTTON AND WOOLEN MILL SUPPLIES. CUTLERY. DRUGS AND MEDICINES—Including, paints, oils, dye-stuffs, surgical instruments and appliances, soaps, perfumes, and toilet articles. *DRY GOODS—Embracing all standard fabrics. ELECTRICAL SUPPLIES. FANCY GOODS AND NOTIONS. FANCY GROCERIES—Including imported delicacies and condiments. FRAMES—Looking-glass and picture. FERTILIZERS. FURNITURE. GROCERIES—Under this head is embraced everything in the grocery line; many articles, such as coffees, sugars, and molasses being of direct importation. GROUND GLUE, VARNISH, TURPENTINE, &C. GUNS AND SPORTING MATERIAL. HARDWARE —Every class. HIDES AND LEATHER. HOUSE FURNISHING GOODS. HARNESS. HATS, CAPS, FURS AND STRAW GOODS. ICE. IRON AND STEEL, LEAD AND COPPER. LADIES' AND GENTS' UNDERWEAR. LIME, PLASTER AND CEMENT. LUBRICATORS—For factories and mills, &c. LUMBER. MACHINIST AND GAS-FITTERS' SUPPLIES. MARBLES. MILLINERY. MUSICAL INSTRUMENTS—Pianos and organs of all the best manufactories—and all smaller instruments. NOTIONS AND HOSIERY— general assortments. NURSERIES. PAPERS—Including book, job, writing, news, card board, &c. PICTURES. PIG-IRON. PLOWS. PORK. POTTERY. PRODUCE. RAILROAD AND MINER'S SUPPLIES. REGALIA. ROOFING. SADDLERY. SASH, BLINDS AND DOORS. SEWING MACHINES —All of the best machines are represented. SILVER-WARE. STOVES AND TIN-WARE. TOBACCO—Plug and smoking and snuff. TOBACCONISTS' SUPPLIES—Including flavorings. TRUNKS AND VALISES. TOYS. WALL PAPERS AND UPHOLSTERING MATERIAL. WATCHES. †WINES AND LIQUORS. WOOD AND WILLOW-WARE. WOOL.

It will be seen from a careful examination of the range of material covered by the foregoing exhibits (manufacturing and jobbing) that it is possible for a merchant to secure in Richmond AN ASSORTED CAR LOAD OF GOODS, and this all merchants who know their business desire to do. The reasons are too obvious to need presentation here.

---

* It is a notable fact that southern fabrics, especially plaids and osnaburgs, are competing on the counters of our wholesale dry goods houses, with the products of the New England mills.

† High grades of direct importation.

CHAPTER VI.

OF INTEREST TO TOURISTS.

HISTORIC—POINTS OF INTEREST IN THE CITY—AS A HOME FOR INVALIDS—THE SCENERY ON THE RAILROAD LINES AND THE SUMMER RESORTS.

Richmond must always possess a fascination for the tourist. As an incorporated place it antedates the Revolutionary period by many years, and has been the scene of many stirring incidents connected with the Colonial period, the Revolution, and the late civil war. Its record is full of historic memories, many of them of the most dramatic character. Its very site was consecrated in blood in the first half of the first century of the Colonial settlement. In 1656, Bloody Run, which marks one of the divides in the eastern plateau of the city, was the scene of a sanguinary engagement between a large force of Richahicrian Indians, and the Border Rangers under Colonel Hill and a band of friendly Indians under Totopotomoi, in which the latter forces were defeated. Shockoe creek, Gillie's creek and Bacon's Quarter Branch are associated with important events of the "Bacon's Rebellion" period in 1676, and in 1781 the city was visited by the British expeditionary force under Arnold and Simcoe, and burned. During the civil war, as the capital of the Confederate Government, it was the great strategic point of attack and defence, the headquarters for the manufacture of all heavy war munitions, and was more than once girdled with fire.

POINTS OF INTEREST.

ST. JOHN'S CHURCH is situated on what is known as Church Hill—a fact which gives the name to that elevation—in the eastern portion of the city, and was built in 1740. It is a quaint, old-fashioned structure, and within its walls Patrick Henry, speaking to the Virginia Convention in 1775, gave utterance to those memorable words: "*Give me liberty, or give me death!*"

RICHMOND, VIRGINIA.   51

The graveyard around it is the resting place of the remains of the older members of many of Richmond's most noted families, and is so filled up that interments cannot now be made without special permission of the City Council.

THE OLD STONE HOUSE is the oldest building of its character in Richmond, dating back to the original settlement. During the revolutionary war it was for a time the headquarters of Washington, and has also been the scene of entertainment of Jefferson, Madison, Lafayette, and other distinguished persons.

THE CAPITOL BUILDING is situated in the Capitol park, or square as it is called by Richmond people, in the centre of the city, and from the top commands a view of the city and surrounding country for miles, in every direction. The corner-stone of the building was laid August the 18th, 1785, and it is the repository of many of Virginia's most valuable relics—Colonial, Revolutionary and Confederate. Among the Colonial relics may be mentioned the records of the Land Office which are continuous from 1620, the chair of the Speaker of the House of Burgesses and the old stove made in England in 1770 by Buzaglo, and presented to the Colony of Virginia by the Duke of Beaufort. This relic is seven feet high, is elaborately ornamented, and up to a few years ago did excellent service in heating the rotunda of the Capitol. In the rotunda is the Houdon statue of Washington—the only authentic statue of Washington in existence, having been modeled from his person—a bust of Lafayette, by the same artist, and a statue of Henry Clay, by Joel T. Hart, which was presented to the State by the ladies of Virginia. In the State Library there are over thirty-five thousand volumes, numerous Colonial manuscripts, and a valuable collection of portraits and busts of distinguished Virginians. The sessions of the convention which passed the ordinance of secession were held in this building, as were also the sessions of the Confederate Congress. The walls of the House of Delegates are ornamented by pictures of Chatham and Jefferson, and those of the Senate chamber by Lami's Storming of a Redoubt at Yorktown and Elder's General R. E. Lee.

THE CAPITOL SQUARE is one of the most beautiful spots in the city. At the highest point in the enclosure is the Washington monument, universally conceded to be the finest monumental group in the country, and one of the finest in the world. The figure of Washington on horseback overlooks and is surrounded by statues of Lewis, Henry, Mason, Jefferson, Marshall and Nelson, which in turn overlook allegorical figures, typifying "Colonial times," "Revolution," "Bill of Rights," "Independence,". "Justice," and "Finance," and the historic events that made these men famous. The figures are of bronze, and the entire cost of the monument was $259,913.61. All of the figures, except those of Lewis, Nelson and Marshall, and the allegorical figures, were designed and executed by Crawford. At his death, the contract for the unfinished work was awarded to Randolph Rogers. Near the Washington monument is the Foley statue of Stonewall Jackson, presented to the State of Virginia by the Right Honorable A. J. Beresford-Hope, and other English gentlemen. A pretty incident connected with this work of art is, that the Boston Knights Templar, during a recent visit to Richmond, marched alone, and unknown to their hosts, from their hotel to the Capitol grounds, and while their band discoursed appropriate music, formed around the statue and decorated it with a wreath of flowers. Within the Capitol enclosure are also the gubernatorial mansion and the old bell-house, which latter, up to the days of reconstruction, served as a guard-house for the State Guard, the standing army of Virginia. This guard did police duty in and about the public buildings. The bell in the tower was used to strike the time, to sound fire-alarms and call out the other military.

THE MONUMENTAL CHURCH is built on the site of the old Richmond Theatre, which was burned December 26, 1811. One hundred and twenty people, including the Governor of the Commonwealth, George W. Smith, perished in the flames. In the portico of the church is a monument on which are recorded the names of the victims.

ST. PAUL'S, the largest Episcopal church in the city, is the edifice in which President Jefferson Davis was seated on Sunday, April 2d, 1865, when the news was received from General Lee sounding the death-knell of the Confederacy.

LIBBY PRISON, now a fertilizer mill, is a plain brick building, situated in the lower part of the city, and was used as a Federal prison during the war.

On BELLE ISLE, a large island in James river, an extensive prison camp was located, and it was this point Dahlgren was endeavoring to reach when he made his celebrated raid.

HOLLYWOOD CEMETERY is on the extreme western edge of the city, and is a place of exceptional natural beauty. Here are buried twelve thousand Confederate soldiers, and here also are located the Monroe monument, and the monument to the Confederate dead, erected by the ladies of the Hollywood Memorial Association. This latter is a granite pyramid 90 feet high. Among other distinguished men buried in Hollywood are John Randolph of Roanoke, Lieutenant-General A. P. Hill, Major-General Geo. Pickett, of Gettysburg fame; Commodore Mathew F. Maury, Governor Henry A. Wise, General J. E. B. Stuart, the cavalry leader, President John Tyler, and others.

OAKWOOD CEMETERY, another beautiful spot, is on the eastern corporation boundary, and the NATIONAL CEMETERY is situated just below the city.

THE FINEST PUBLIC BUILDINGS are the Custom-House and Post-Office, the Medical College, and the Almshouse. The City Hall, a striking Doric structure, was condemned and pulled down as insecure, but the people of the city have voted to erect a new one at a cost of $300,000. The Medical College is a State institution of the highest repute at home and abroad. The faculty embraces some of the most eminent physicians in Richmond, and its clinical advantages are very superior.

THE CONFEDERATE WHITE HOUSE.—The mansion occupied by President Davis during the war is a substantial building erected by an opulent gentleman for a private residence. It is now used as a public school. THE LEE HOUSE is on the most fashionable thoroughfare and is a commodious but unpretentious building.

VALENTINE'S STUDIO attracts a large number of visitors. Here, in addition to the original casts of the artist's own works —prominent among them the recumbent figure of General R. E. Lee—are numerous examples of the plastic art from abroad. In the neighborhood of Valentine's studio is the residence of Chief Justice John Marshall.

THE RICHMOND COLLEGE grounds and buildings are situated

near the western boundary of the city at the head of one of the most fashionable avenues. The institution is in a flourishing condition, and is accumulating a valuable museum.

The Battle-fields around Richmond are objects of interest to tourists from all parts of the country, and many of the earthworks thrown up on them are still standing. They are approached from the city by good roads. The more generally visited points are Seven Pines, Cold Harbor, Mechanicsville, Fort Harrison, Malvern Hill, Savage's Station and Drewry's Bluff. Savage Station can also be reached by the Richmond, York River and Chesapeake Railroad, and Drewry's Bluff by the river. This latter stronghold was the scene of the unsuccessful attack, made May 16, 1862, by the Union fleet, consisting of the Monitor, Galena, Aroostook, Naugatuck, Port Royal and other vessels.

FOR INVALIDS.

Richmond is the great intermediate stopping-place for travellers between Florida and the North, and is highly commended as a winter residence for those fleeing the more rigorous climate of the latter section. The winters are mild, and in the late spring the city is truly a city of foliage and flowers. So much of the travel alluded to passes through here that it is in contemplation to erect a handsome hotel in the fashionable part of the city for its especial accommodation. Regardless of this improvement, however, there is room for the profitable investment of capital in another hotel. As before stated, the people extend the warmest welcome to strangers, and already there is a large resident northern element. As a diverging point for tourists it also possesses great advantages. A few hours' ride by any line of transportation brings complete change of scenery, and on every route, water or rail, there are points of interest worth especial trips.

JAMES RIVER ROUTE.

The banks of the river from Richmond to Norfolk are studded on both sides with historical localities. Powhatan, in sight of the city, is the site of one of the residences of the Indian king by that name, whose daughter saved the life of Captain John Smith. She stands in Virginia's history as an Indian princess and the maternal ancestor of some of the most prominent people in the State. WHITBY was settled as early as 1620, only thirteen years after JAMESTOWN, and WARWICK, only four miles below Richmond, was before the Revolution the shipping point for the city. Passing AMPTHILL, the residence of a celebrated Colonial patriot, FALLING CREEK, on which is the site of the first iron furnace erected in the Colony, DREWRY'S and CHAFFIN'S BLUFFS, we come to DUTCH GAP. Here the river makes a long sweep around a narrow neck of land, known as Farrar's Island, and here General B. F. Butler in 1864 undertook to cut his canal, with a view of protecting the Federal gunboats from the heavy fire of the Confederate batteries. After the war the work was completed by the United States government, in the interest of commerce, and has proved a great advantage to the city, as it cuts off seven miles of very tedious navigation. Between Dutch Gap and FORT POWHATAN, built during the Revolution by order of Baron Steuben, may be noted VARINA and CURL'S NECK, Colonial residences; TURKEY BEND, where General McClellan took refuge under cover of his gunboats after the seven days' fight; MALVERN HILL, SHIRLEY and BERKELEY, fine old Colonial homesteads—the latter the birthplace of President Harrison; WESTOVER, the seat of William Byrd, the founder of Richmond and Petersburg; WILCOX'S, where General Grant crossed the James on his movement from Spotsylvania Courthouse to Petersburg, and WEYANOKE, another Colonial homestead, and the scene of a massacre of the settlers by the Indians. UPPER BRANDON, LOWER BRANDON and SANDY POINT, Colonial residences, follow next, and then comes JAMESTOWN, or "James Cittie," the first capital of the Colony, and the seat of the residences of the Royal Governors of Virginia. In 1619 the first legislative assembly in America met at Jamestown and until 1676 it continued to be the scene of all the pomp and ceremony of a court in minature. In that year, however—during Bacon's Rebellion—it was burned, and began to decline, and now all that marks the spot is the tower of the old church in which Pocahontas was baptized and married, and the graveyard surrounding it. Just below Jamestown is KING'S MILL WHARF, the landing for WILLIAMSBURG, four miles distant, to which the capital of the

Colony was removed in 1698, and where Spotswood and his successors reigned in vice-regal splendor until the voice of Henry sounded the key-note of revolution. Williamsburg was settled in 1632 and is the seat of the venerable COLLEGE OF WILLIAM AND MARY, founded in 1692, and the oldest seat of learning in the United States except Harvard. Among the other reminders of the Colonial period yet to be seen are the remains of the Governor's palace, the Powder-horn, and the House of Burgesses, where Henry made his great speech ending, "*If this be treason make the most of it.*" The parish church, one of the oldest church edifices in Virginia, is in an excellent state of preservation. Williamsburg can also be reached by the Newports News branch of the Chesapeake and Ohio railway. Off NEWPORTS NEWS, the next point of interest, the naval engagement between the Confederate ram Virginia (or Merrimac) and the steamers Patrick Henry and Jamestown and two or three small gunboats, and the United States fleet of wooden vessels took place March 8, 1862, and the following day in the same waters occurred the fight between the Virginia and the Monitor. At OLD POINT COMFORT are the Hygeia hotel, a favorite summer resort and winter sanitarium, and FORTRESS MONROE, the largest and strongest fortress in this country. Near Fortress Monroe is the town of HAMPTON, famous in Colonial, Revolutionary and Confederate history. It is the seat of the Hampton Normal and Agricultural Institute, and the location of one of the oldest churches in the United States. The marshes and reaches of James river abound in water fowl, affording excellent sport and are much frequented by Northern sportsmen.

THE CHESAPEAKE AND OHIO ROUTE.

Hanover courthouse is the first place of note after leaving Richmond on the road going west. The old courthouse was erected in 1735, of imported brick, and is memorable for its colonial and revolutionary reminiscences. Gordonsville is the first large town, but before reaching it Trevillian's station is passed, and near this point is the MILITARY ROAD cut by Lafayette when in pursuit of the British in 1781. Shadwell, 93 miles from Richmond, is the site of the old mill property of Thomas

Jefferson (the ruins are still standing), and two miles further west the traveller comes in sight of MONTICELLO, the famous retreat and burial-place of the great commoner. Charlottesville is next, and a mile beyond is the UNIVERSITY OF VIRGINIA, the beautiful grounds and buildings of which are in full view of the railroad. This institution, the "child of Mr. Jefferson's old age," was founded in 1819, in pursuance of a long cherished idea, and formally opened March 7, 1825. Mr. Jefferson superintended every detail of the construction of the buildings, importing artizans to do some of the finer work. It is liberally endowed by the State of Virginia, and has always stood in the front rank of the educational institutions of the country. Among its *post. bellum* benefactors may be mentioned the Honorable W. W. Corcoran, of Washington, W. H. Vanderbilt, of New York city, and the late Lewis Brooks, of Rochester. To Mr. Brooks it owes its handsome museum building and the splendid collection it contains Through the liberality of Mr. Leander McCormick, of Chicago, it also possesses a magnificent observatory. The University draws its patronage from all parts of the country, and its alumni have distinguished themselves in all walks of life. It may be mentioned here, as an evidence of the abatement of sectional feeling, that not only are the University and other educational institutions receiving students from the North, but that boys are being prepared in our private schools for these institutions. From Mechum's river, ten miles west of the University, the road begins the ascent of the eastern slope of the Blue Ridge, tunnelling the mountains at Rockfish gap. This point is 1,500 above tide-level and the windings of the road before reaching the tunnel command a view of one of the most picturesque landscapes in this country. From the western mouth of the tunnel, the road descends into the Valley of Virginia, connecting at Waynesboro with the Shenandoah Valley Railroad for Luray Caverns—conceded to be among the most remarkable cave-formations in the world. Staunton, 136 miles from Richmond, is the seat of four of the largest female educational institutions in the South—the Augusta Female Seminary (Presbyterian), the Virginia Female Institute (Episcopal), the Wesleyan Female Institute (Methodist), and Staunton Female Seminary (Lutheran). It is a place remarkable for its health, and is the junction of the

Valley and the Chesapeake and Ohio railroads. At this point the traveller makes railroad or stage connection for Stribling Springs, Weyer's Cave, the Cave of the Fountains, and Rawley, Orkney, and Capon Springs. A few miles west of Staunton the road enters what is termed the great mineral spring basin of Virginia and West Virginia, in which are situated the following well known summer resorts: Variety Springs, Crawford Springs, Cold Sulphur Springs, Rockbridge Baths, Rockbridge Alum and Jordan Alum Springs, Millboro' Springs, Wallawhatoola Springs, the Warm, Hot and Healing Springs, Dagger's Springs, the Old Sweet and the Sweet Chalybeate Springs, the Salt Sulphur, the Red Sulphur, and the Greenbrier White Sulphur Springs. The distance from Staunton to the White Sulphur is 91 miles, and the distance from the White Sulphur to Huntington is 194 miles, much of the road being through a country unequalled for wildness and grandeur of scenery, and involving feats of engineering as difficult as any ever attempted on this continent. The Rev. John Hall, D. D , in a letter to a New York paper describing his trip over the road, says:

"My way lay along the line of the Chesapeake and Ohio railroad, and he who can travel by it unmoved ought to be placed permanently on the Jersey flats, and forbidden the sight of anything more picturesque than a machine shop. There is a famous road in Italy which attracts by its rapid alternations of dark tunnel and picturesque valley; but it is no exaggeration to say that as much could be abstracted from the Virginia line without being missed. Every one who ever crossed the Alps into Italy remembers the zigzags from which he looks down on the valley he is reaching. But the hills around are bare and hard. The generous Alleghanies and the Blue Ridge are richly wooded to their tops, and look as soft and green as the hill-sides around Lake Maggiore. All travellers by the Pennsylvania Central remember that attractive piece of fancy engineering known as the Horse-Shoe, and nobody has gone to California without recalling the doubling of Cape Horn—where your train winds round the high brow of a mountain, as if it had climbed up to give you a look at the valleys below. The traveller across the Virginias can have delights like these again and again repeated. The Rhine owes no little of its attractiveness to the battlements on its steeps. The New river is not, indeed, like the Rhine in depth or breadth, but it has features of its own. Now it is a broad stream, leisurely chattering to the woods that overhang it; anon it is in a narrower bed scolding the rocks as large as houses, that have intruded themselves upon it from the hill-sides, of which they grew weary. But for giant cliffs, Eagle's Nests, Lover's Leaps, Drachenfels, and mountain fastnesses in ruins, the New river can compete with any stream of travelled lands, and with this difference in its favor, that no cunning count or baron bold piled up those frowning battlements. Geological forces in an Omnipotent hand, and with an unlimited time in which to work, placed these precipitous, castle-like crowns on the wooded hills, and gave them a peculiarity not seen elsewhere—namely: that behind them corn and wine abound; for the Alleghanies are fertile to their summits. As one is whirled along, it is difficult to say which challenges most admiration—the river below, the cliffs above, the graceful lines of the hills, the moving shadows over the green slopes of the mountain sides, or the sublime audacity that dared to run a railroad through such a region."

RICHMOND AND ALLEGHANY ROUTE.

This road traverses the beautiful James River valley for 230 miles. There is hardly a foot of the distance that is not picturesque and the traveler is seldom if ever out of sight of the river. From Richmond to Lynchburg, 146 miles, the valley is very wide, the farm-lands are in a very high state of cultivation, the elevations at many points are crowned by handsome country seats, and the ponds formed by the dams of the old canal company present the appearance of a series of lakes. Beyond Lynchburg the line strikes into the mountainous regions and the scenery is exceedingly grand. For long stretches it hugs the bluffs on one side while the river foams and eddies and dashes over its rocky bed on the other. At Balcony Falls where the James river bursts through the Blue Ridge and the mountains rise a thousand feet from the water's edge, the line divides—one branch taking the bank of North river to Lexington, and the other continuing, as before described, along the James, *via* the Natural Bridge to Buchanan, and thence to Clifton Forge. This latter place marks the water-gap cut through the prolongation of Richpatch mountain, and through which flow the waters of the Jackson fork of the James river. The cliffs on either side of the river are nearly perpendicular, suggesting the idea that some mighty convulsion of nature has cleft the mountain in twain, while high up on either bluff, the peculiar geological formation gives a perfect arch. Lexington is noted as a centre of education, and is one of the prettiest and healthiest towns in the State.

Here are located WASHINGTON AND LEE UNIVERSITY, the VIRGINIA MILITARY INSTITUTE, and the ANN SMITH FEMALE ACADEMY. The first-named was founded in 1749, as Augusta Academy. In 1777, it was removed to the vicinity of Lexington,. and in 1796,* it was endowed by General Washington, with a view to making it a national school and named Washington Academy,† and in 1812 was organized under a new charter as Washington College. Its alumni embrace some of the most distinguished Virginians of the past and present. Subsequently it was further endowed by Light-Horse Harry Lee, John Robinson, a distinguished soldier of the Revolution, and friend of Washington, and the Society of the Cincinnati. At the close of the late civil war, General R. E. Lee was called to the Presidency of the institution, in which position he remained until his. death. He was succeeded by his son, General G. W. C. Lee, and in 1871, the name of the Institution was changed to Washington

---

* Between the two last dates it was known as Liberty Hall Academy,. and its rector, William Graham, made a northern tour in its interest "as far as Boston, collecting 776 pounds and 18 shillings." During Tarleton's demonstration, when the General Assembly was driven from the low country towards the mountains, the rector and his boys marched to Rockfish Gap to dispute the passage of the Blue Ridge. Priestly, the distinguished teacher of Tennessee, and Alexander of Princeton, were pupils at Liberty Hall Academy.

† General Washington, in reply to a letter from Samuel Houston, clerk of the Board acknowledging the endowment (which at this day yields 6 per cent. on $50,000), wrote as follows:

"MOUNT VERNON, June 17, 1798.

"GENTLEMEN—Unaccountable as it may seem, it is nevertheless true, that the address with which you were pleased to honor me—dated the 12th of April—never came to my hands until the 14th instant.

"To promote literature in this rising Empire, and to encourage the Arts, have ever been amongst the warmest wishes of my heart. And if the donation which the generosity of the Legislature of the Commonwealth of Virginia has enabled me to bestow on Liberty Hall, now by your politeness called Washington Academy, is likely to prove a mean to accomplish these ends, it will contribute to the gratification of my desires. Sentiments like those which have flowed from your pen excite my gratitude, whilst I offer my best vows for the prosperity of the Academy, and for the honor and happiness of those under whose auspices it is conducted.

"GEORGE WASHINGTON."

and Lee University. Of late years the endowment fund has been greatly increased, through the munificence of friends, both North and South, who desire to carry out Washington's idea of a national seat of learning. Among the most prominent benefactors may be mentioned Honorable Cyrus McCormick, of Chicago, the late Warren Newcomb, of New York, Hon. W. W. Corcoran, of Washington, the late Honorable George Peabody, the late Col. Thomas Scott and H. H. Houston, Esq., of Philadelphia, R. H. Bayly, Esq., of New Orleans, and the late Lewis Brooks, of Rochester, and others. A number of scholarships also have been founded by Northern ladies and gentlemen, and the widow of Mr. Newcomb has recently erected on the college grounds, as a memorial to her husband, a new library building at a cost of $20,000. The course is on the most advanced plane. . The VIRGINIA MILITARY INSTITUTE was founded in 1839, is endowed by the State, and has a reputation for thoroughness of work not second to that of the National Military Academy. In this institution were educated many of the prominent officers of the Confederate army, and it was through the Institute boys as drill-masters that Virginia was able to put an army in the field so soon after the secession of the State. Five of its professors and two hundred of its alumni were slain in battle in the late civil war, and three hundred and fifty of its alumni wounded. The buildings were burned during General Hunter's raid, but have been rebuilt according to the original plan. Stonewall Jackson was a professor in the Military Institute at the breaking out of the civil war, and his remains are buried in the Lexington cemetery. The remains of General Lee and wife and daughter rest temporarily beneath the floor of Washington and Lee University chapel, but are to be removed to the crypt beneath the Lee mausoleum—an annex to the chapel—which will contain Valentine's marble recumbent figure of the Confederate chieftain. This is Mr. Valentine's *chef d'œuvre*, and will be unveiled in June next. The Ann Smith Academy is a venerable institution, enjoying a reputation all over the State. From Lexington there is stage connection to Goshen, on the Chesapeake and Ohio railway, and through Goshen Pass, noted for the beauty of its scenery. There is also stage service to the Natural Bridge, where, it may be noted, a fine park has been laid out, and new hotels have lately been erected. The tributaries of the James river, as do all the mountain streams of Virginia, abound in food fishes, especially the black bass and trout, and in the mountains themselves are found deer, bear, wild turkeys, pheasants, and other game.

RICHMOND AND DANVILLE ROUTE.

The Richmond and Danville system is the most direct route to the Buffalo Lithia Springs, a noted health resort in Virginia, and the resorts of Northeast Georgia, Upper South Carolina, and Western North Carolina which, until late years, constituted a *terra incognita* to the outside world. In Northeast Georgia and Western North Carolina, particularly, the scenery is grand beyond description, abounding as it does in towering mountains, rapid torrents, and dizzy waterfalls. The country is also rich in Indian lore. In Georgia there are the White Sulphur Springs, the Lodge Rock, Mount Airy, Tallulah Falls, the Grand Chasm, Toccoa Falls; and in North Carolina—Cullisaja Falls, Catalouche Canyon, Sugar Fork Falls, the scenes on the French Broad, Piedmont Springs, Warm Springs, Mount Mitchell, Mount Pisgah, and other points well worthy of a special visit. The scenery about Asheville has caused that country to be most properly named the "Switzerland of America." On the Richmond, Chesapeake and York River division of this system the tourist leaving Richmond, passes Savage Station or Fair Oaks, and taking the boat at West Point proceeds to Yorktown, the scene of Lord Cornwallis's surrender.

THE RICHMOND AND FREDERICKSBURG ROUTE.

The Richmond and Fredericksburg is the favorite line for tourists from the North coming to Richmond. At Washington they have the option of taking the boat down the Potomac river, and passing in full view of Mount Vernon—or the Pennsylvania All-rail Connection to Quantico. At and near the old city of Fredericksburg are some of the most noted battle-fields of the war. Ashland, 16 miles from Richmond, is the principal town between Fredericksburg and Richmond, is but a short distance from the birthplace of Henry Clay, and is the seat of Randolph Macon College. This Institution was founded in 1832, by the Methodist denomination, and is in a flourishing condition. Ashland is also the residence of numbers of Richmond business men. The Virginia Theological Seminary (Episcopal), organized in 1827, is located at Alexandria, Virginia, on the line of this system, between Richmond and Washington. There has been only one fatal accident on this road—the oldest road in the State—and that was not the fault of the company.

THE COAST-LINE ROUTE.

Twenty-two miles from Richmond the Coast-line route passes through Petersburg, thence on to the Seaside resorts of North Carolina and the orange groves of Florida. Petersburg is a city of 22,000 inhabitants. The country around it was the scene of some of the most desperate fighting of the war, and many of the houses in the city bear the marks of Federal shells to this day. The "Crater" battle-field is one of the objects of especial interest connected with those dark days, and the colonial period is represented in the picturesque ruins of old Blandford church. From Petersburg it is but a short ride by rail over the Norfolk and Western road to the edge of the famous Dismal Swamp.

THE NORFOLK AND WESTERN ROUTE.

Connection is made with the Norfolk and Western route by either the Petersburg, the Danville, or the Richmond and Alleghany. From Burkeville, the point of connection with the Danville road to Lynchburg, the route passes through much of the territory over which General Lee's army made its retreat to Appomattox Courthouse, the scene of the surrender. Farmville, in Prince Edward county, is the depot for Hampden Sidney, the seat of Hampden Sidney College and Union Theological Seminary. The former was organized in 1775 under Presbyterian auspices, the latter in 1824. Both schools have a widespread and enviable reputation. West of Lynchburg the objects of interests for tourists, pleasure and health seekers reached by the road are Blue Ridge Springs, Coyner's Springs, the Peaks of Otter, Salt Pond, Bedford Alum Springs, Bald Knob, the Natural Tunnel, Botetourt Springs (the seat of Hollins (Female) Institute), Roanoke Red Sulphur Springs, Montgomery White Sulphur Springs, the Yellow Sulphur Springs, Pulaski Alum

Springs, New River White Sulphur Springs, Sharon Springs, and Alleghany Springs. At Salem is located Roanoke College, organized under Lutheran patronage in 1853; and at Emory, Emory and Henry College, organized in 1837. The Virginia Agricultural and Mechanical College, a State institution, is situated at Blacksburg, on this route.

CONCLUSION.

In conclusion and *apropos* of summer resorts and excursions let us again say a word to artizans and others whose means will not allow them to avail themselves of the fashionable places of recreation. The heated term in Richmond does not necessitate a general exodus, and even when it becomes desirable to have a change of air, going into the country does not involve a long and expensive trip. The gates of the city literally open out upon pastures green and running streams—a buggy ride of a couple of miles in any direction from the corporation line and the country is spread before us in all of its freshness. The towns and villages of the State are far between, and on all the railroad routes we have described there are numerous farm houses where good board can be obtained at reasonable rates, and every necessary accommodation is found. The country folk of Virginia, while they cannot, as a rule, afford to keep open houses, as they did before the war, have lost none of their hospitality or faculty for making strangers feel at home, and for this reason many families of abundant means prefer the quiet farm-house, for spending the summer, to the public resorts.

www.ingramcontent.com/pod-product-compliance
Lightning Source LLC
Chambersburg PA
CBHW022145090426
42742CB00010B/1401